MY
CITY
OF
FUSI●N

by **Patrick Chu**

**East Meets West and
Past Meets Future**

THE UNIQUE STORY OF HONG KONG

Typeset in Athelas

Editing, design, typesetting and publishing by UK Book Publishing

www.ukbookpublishing.com

ISBN: 978-1-914195-66-2

*Dedicated to all those who work and live in Hong Kong
and those who will work and live in Hong Kong*

CONTENTS

MY CITY OF FUSION

East meets West and Past meets Future

INTRODUCTION
Hong Kong and I

Hong Kong is a small city, but it is a great city. It has a mixture of Eastern and Western cultures because of its unique history. It is, quite arguably, one of the most unusual places in the history of the modern world.

Hong Kong should be seen as a blessed city in China, inhabited by blessed people who all should claim credit to its success. However, I cannot myself claim credit for being part of this success story of Hong Kong as I left in 1980, just before Hong Kong entered its Golden Era. Nonetheless, I wanted to feel and share the joy of seeing this success, with great pride and satisfaction, even as a bystander. The many achievements of the people of Hong Kong, despite the turbulence they have gone through, particularly the period of hardship at the beginning of the post- WW2 period, cannot be overstated.

Hong Kong has a unique place in the history of colonialism. It started as a British colony, way back in 1842. Yet, unlike other colonies which previously belonged to the British Empire in the post- WW2 world, when it was standard post- WW2 British policy to grant independence to its many colonies, Hong Kong was reunited with its motherland China after more than 150 years of separation.

It is also a very prosperous and a popular city. It can offer, quite possibly, the only experience of sampling the cultural mix between the East and the West. Nearly all travellers who have visited Hong Kong in the last 50 years are likely to concur with these views. This is why Hong Kong still remains as one of the most popular tourist attractions in the world.

In 2018, there were 65 million visitors to Hong Kong, of which a staggering 51 million were tourists coming from mainland China. It has always been a popular holiday destination for the mainland Chinese to visit Hong Kong, mainly due to its attraction of shopping and its feel of modernity. Deep down inside the psyche of the tourists from China, I imagine there could be an undefinable yearn and curiosity to see how the only colony ceded by China to the British Empire two centuries ago has turned out. After all, this was a colony where more than 90% of the local residents are still ethnic Chinese. They may dress differently, talk differently, but are unmistakably ethnic Chinese nonetheless!

Most of the travellers who come over stay here for a short period, combining sightseeing and shopping. The location of Hong Kong serves also as an ideal stopover for those tourists who may choose a more extensive holiday either in the rest of Asia or mainland China, and thus Hong Kong has always been an integral part of any travelling itinerary in Asia.

This unique background is what makes the story of Hong Kong so fascinating. I believe, even the most far-sighted naval officers serving in the British naval fleet, at the height of the power of the British Empire, could never have imagined that what was then viewed as a few barren rocks called Hong Kong, intended to be used as a trading stopover for Britain, would become the Hong Kong of today.

The metamorphosis and transformation of Hong Kong started in earnest after WW2. At the time, Britain had a few colonies scattered in various parts of the world, from Southeast Asia to the West Indies, but Hong Kong stood out distinctly. The British people have always regarded the jewel of the crown in the British Empire to be India, due to its vast size, population, and the British Raj, but dare I say the second jewel of the crown must be Hong Kong. In fact, after WW2, Hong Kong might very well be the only jewel left in the British Empire.

The change, therefore, from the status of Hong Kong as a colony to being handed back to China in 1997, was an unprecedented political event in modern history, in which a colonial power, instead of granting independence to the colony, actually handed back the sovereignty of the colony to its mother country, through a process of negotiations.

Furthermore, it is my view that there is not a single city in the world which can be remotely compared to Hong Kong in terms of the historical landscape it found itself in, and built itself up to be such a city of international relevance and significance in a time span of just over 70 years, starting from 1945.

In modern day Hong Kong, there is now a rich tapestry of diversified cultures, the emergence of which is what makes Hong Kong tick and what makes Hong Kong so interesting. The cultures can be ethnic culture, religious culture, political culture and popular culture. When we visit restaurants anywhere in the world these days, we often see the word 'fusion', which is used to mean the menu can offer a mixture of the cuisines from various cultures to the customers. Following this line of thinking, Hong Kong is quite possibly the original fusion city before the word fusion became fashionable.

Hong Kong, in the early 1960s, used to be called a Borrowed Place on Borrowed Time. This of course referred to the colonial acquisition of the Hong Kong Island from 1842 with the signing of the Nanking Treaty following the defeat of China in the Opium War by the Royal British Navy, at the height of the British Empire in the 19th century. However, one needs to be more specific here. Even though it is conventionally accepted to think of Hong Kong being ceded to the British as a colony in 1842, that actually refers only to Hong Kong Island, which has an area of merely 80 square kilometres. Then in 1860, this colony of the Hong Kong Island was extended with the addition of the Kowloon Peninsula following the second Opium War. In 1898, the Second Convention of Peking further expanded the colony with the 99-year lease of the New Territories, covering an area north of the Kowloon Peninsula defined by the aptly named Boundary Street.

It is this lease of the New Territories, added to Hong Kong Island and Kowloon Peninsula, that formed the basis of the views adopted by many commentators and historians who coined the idea that the existence of Hong Kong was a Borrowed Place on Borrowed Time.

These days, when we talk about Hong Kong, it actually encompasses the whole of Hong Kong as it is commonly known, covering a total area of about 1,000 square kilometres. The New Territories alone accounted for 953 square kilometres. Though these three areas were conceded or leased to the British, for practical purposes the three areas have been collectively known as Hong Kong since 1898. Hence, the British colonial administration had always governed the three areas as one single colonial entity.

The UK took administrative responsibility for Hong Kong by appointing a governor from London ever since Hong Kong was ceded to the British Empire, except for the period of Japanese occupation during WW2 for three years and eight months from December 1941 to August 1945.

On July 1, 1997 Hong Kong was returned to China under the One Country Two Systems principle of governing Hong Kong, pioneered by Deng Xiaoping, who was then the paramount leader of China. The Chinese government replaced the governor with the appointment of, through an electoral assembly, a Chief Executive of the Hong Kong Special Administrative Region (HKSAR) who is charged with the special administrative responsibilities of running Hong Kong.

This great and rich city came through the last 150 years not without difficulties. It has certainly not been plain sailing. Yet, each time Hong Kong, when faced with such challenges, was able to rise up again and emerge stronger than before. These challenges included WW2, when Hong Kong was under Japanese occupation for over three years. Then there were the 1956 riots, the 1967 riots, the very unsettling times during the Sino-British talks on the future of Hong Kong in 1982, the Asian financial crisis in 1997/98, SARS (Severe Acute Respiratory Syndrome) in 2003, the global financial crisis in 2008, the umbrella movement in 2014, anti-extradition protests in 2019, followed by the Covid-19 pandemic in 2020.

These crises caused significant difficulties for the people of Hong Kong. The nature of these crises varied from being political or financial, to health and social, some of which were even repetitive in nature. They led to much hardship for the people of Hong Kong, especially the poor, and an uncertain future for the young, and at times, even brain drain when the skilled and educated ventured abroad to build a new life. Yet, despite these difficulties, Hong Kong came good every time and its economic growth only dipped into the negative territory on three occasions in the last 40 years! These were during the speculative Asian Financial Crisis of 1997/98, the health crisis SARS of 2003, and the anti-extradition protests and the Covid-19 pandemic in 2019/2020.

It is remarkable that the people of Hong Kong emerged smarter and stronger with each crisis. As Hong Kong became more and more prosperous, it also became a more outward-looking, open society. The people of Hong Kong became kinder, gentler and more civil. Further elaboration of this important point will follow later in the ensuing chapters where the charitable work in Hong Kong is discussed. Since Hong Kong has always been a tariff-free port open to commerce and trade, this combination of openness and civility all led to the formation of a modern society with a quiet and unassuming display of human decency and a unique social harmony that few places can match.

For sure, Hong Kong is not without any failings. While Hong Kong boasts one of the highest net asset wealth of individuals in the world, and, according to information published in The Asset, a financial magazine for Asia, the average wealth per adult in Hong Kong in 2019 was estimated at US$489,260 (compared to a global average of US$70,850). Yet Hong Kong also had a Gini index of 0.54, indicating that the majority of wealth was concentrated on fewer people, leading to a high degree of income inequality. Indeed, over the last 40 years, this coefficient for Hong Kong has gradually increased, suggesting a gradual trend towards greater income inequality. So, one of the problems, and indeed the main criticism of Hong Kong from the liberal economists, is that in spite of its wealth, there is a wider gap of income inequality compared with other Western countries of similar wealth. There are still many poor people who are not quite able to share the riches. This also leads directly to another failing, which is high property prices and rental costs at levels that fewer and fewer people can afford. This disparity has become more acute in recent years. There is another problem, which is a sort of time bomb ticking away. This is the demographic situation of a rapidly ageing population, with Hong Kong now having the highest life expectancy for both men and women in the world.

The above is a very brief and short history of Hong Kong, touching only lightly on its successes, its challenges and even its failings. It would be of some relevance to the readers at this point that I should say something about myself.

My life can be divided into three stages. The first third was my formative years, up to the completion of my tertiary education. This lasted about 24 years. The middle third was spent entirely in the UK where I became a haematologist. This lasted for about 32 years. During this period, I came back to visit Hong Kong at least once a year to see my mother, my brother, sisters and their families. The third part was my work in Shenzhen, a city in southern China, just north of the border with Hong Kong, as a medical doctor at the University of Hong Kong Shenzhen Hospital (HKU SZH) in the last nine years. I reached my retirement age of 65 in 2019 and started to write my first book which was then published in 2020. It was mainly about my experiences of working at HKU SZH. Then early January 2020 came Covid-19, which changed the world. I wrote my second book in May 2020 on the experience I had in dealing with Covid-19 in China.

For nearly the whole of 2020, the world was engaged in fighting the Covid-19 pandemic and one key universal advice to everyone is social distancing. Everyone should stay at home as much as one can. This is indeed one of the most effective ways of protecting the public, as well as protecting oneself, from the infection, in the absence of an effective vaccine. This combination of being semi-retired and the need for strict social distancing gave me time to think, to learn and to make up for the lost time in doing the things I ought to be doing.

I started thinking about the idea of this book in July 2020. I knew it was going to be very difficult, perhaps even controversial, and some would say it is untimely. The whole world was in turmoil with the Covid-19 pandemic. Governments were struggling to cope, and people were in despair. Meanwhile, the two biggest economies in the world, the US and China, were, for lack of a better word, squaring up to each other on their political, economic and ideological differences. This is worrying as they are the two biggest and most powerful countries in the world. In July, Hong Kong itself was gripped in the midst of another wave of Covid-19 infections and also had to face the introduction on July 1, 2020 of the new National Security Law legislated in China for Hong Kong in May 2020.

No one knows how these tensions and problems will play out. Even though vaccines were available towards the end of 2020, the future is still uncertain and to some, deeply worrying. In Hong Kong, once again, the hot topic which was commonly seen in print in the press and social media was emigration. Having made the move to the UK way back in 1980, I firmly believe that emigration is something easier to think of and even talk about, uncomfortable though it may be, but extremely difficult to carry out. It replaces one set of uncertainties with another. Not only are there many known unknowns, worse still, there can be many unknown unknowns. We all wish we can move to what we perceive to be a better place, but when we dig deep, we start to wonder where this better place will be, never mind the how.

Even though I have spent a good part of my life away from Hong Kong, I have always maintained a close personal interest in events in Hong Kong over the last few decades. I have never been too detached or disconnected from Hong Kong. Though my home is now in the UK, Hong Kong is still where my ageing mum in her 90s is, where my brother and sisters are, the in-laws, and the school friends.

Since 2012, I have worked in China and started shuttling weekly between Shenzhen and Hong Kong, which is about a 35-minute train journey away, very similar to Liverpool and Manchester in the UK. This period of working in China gave me the unique opportunity to get to know China better and appreciate the role Hong Kong can play in the modernization of China. A feeling of familiarity with Hong Kong resurfaced in me, as well as me developing a new feeling of acquaintance with life in China, especially in the city of Shenzhen.

I was in the UK in the summer of 2020, unable to go back to China to resume my work at the hospital, due to the 14+14 days of mandatory quarantine (14 days on entering Hong Kong, then another 14 days on entering China). During this period of enforced social isolation because of Covid-19, I started to ask myself an honest question. Since the future is indeed uncertain, and many people in Hong Kong felt that they were at a crossroads, can I at least attempt to see a way through by thinking more in depth about the recent past of Hong Kong? In other words, can the past serve as a guide to the future? My gut feeling is that it can, as history can always, if for nothing else, serve as a pointer for us all. Would my own past and experience help to shed some light for the others on how we deal with the future with fewer uncertainties? Since I was brought up in Hong Kong from the age of three, and spent the first quarter of my life there, was there anything I could write about this city, which I have come to love and admire? In doing so, how should I best share my sentiments for this city with the readers?

As I contemplated, cogitated, deliberated if I had enough in me even to attempt to write such a book, I started to delve deeply into my memory bank, and do some research as well. I found that there was no shortage of books written in English about Hong Kong. Some were novels with settings in Hong Kong (some of which I have even read), some were travel guides, and some were non-fictions mainly about events in Hong Kong at the time when the UK was negotiating with China on how Hong Kong should be handed back to China, and a few were on the history of Hong Kong up to the early 2010s.

Many recent books, especially those published in English, seemed to be focusing on political events and their implications since the civil unrest in Hong Kong in 2014. Interestingly, there seems to be a shortage of books based primarily on a narrative on the social, economic and cultural successes of Hong Kong, and its shortcomings from WW2 right up to 2020. In other words, how my generation (which of course does not include me personally as I had been away), known collectively as the post-war baby boomers, have played their parts in Hong Kong. The few books that are available are of fine scholarly achievement, but regrettably the last one was published in 1997, the year that Hong Kong was handed back to China by the UK. Some books since have also been published, but these are mainly aimed at the HKSAR administration and governance, or at the two major protest movements, the first in 2014 and the second in 2019.

The lack of a narrative for the period stretching from the 1950s to the present days of 2021 was the main reason for me to write this book.

Furthermore, I also think that the stance that some of these books took was too negative, perhaps even overcritical of Hong Kong, with little attention paid to the achievements of Hong Kong in the last few decades and, in particular, how the people of Hong Kong have all contributed to the success and even more, how the joy of the success was shared out among the local people. So, in this regard, this book also tells their story for them, especially by someone like me who can claim no credit for this success. There was hardly any book which commented on the seminal events in Hong Kong in a setting which is calibrated against the global landscapes, such as the dominance of free market economics, the modernization of China, the emergence of the many successful Asian economies in the world and, more importantly, on the transition of Hong Kong from being a British colony to being part of China since 1997, which in itself is a milestone event in its audacity, originality and economic significance.

It can be very difficult for me to explain to the readers why I plucked up enough courage to write this book. What purpose would it serve? I am not a professional writer (to even see myself as an amateurish writer is to compliment myself in a way I hardly deserve), nor a political commentator, nor a social scientist, and certainly not a historian. So, I really have nothing of any value to contribute, some people might say, and indeed they may be right. The only thing I can say for myself is that I have taken a more than passing interest in Hong Kong and China all these years, even when I was in the UK. Along with many other people of Hong Kong, there are things that I saw, things I experienced and have developed some sentiments for. I wish to share with the readers my sentiments of various events in Hong Kong, recollected and remembered over many years. In so doing, perhaps it is possible that I can tell a story of relevance, dare I say, of Hong Kong.

I am therefore hoping that these personal recollections of Hong Kong can paint for the readers an image of Hong Kong, for better or for worse, which can be told and perhaps even retold, among the readers in a distinctive and semi-personal way. In other words, this is a sort of brief memoir of my own life in Hong Kong to share with the readers. I sincerely hope that it can lead to a better understanding and appreciation of this city of just over 1,000 square kilometres, not only as a British colony in its past history, but also presently as an important part of China.

At the time of starting this book, the UK was coming out of the first wave of Covid-19. The country was unlocked after the first national lockdown but social distancing and self-isolation were still very much part of the government advice to prevent further waves. The New Normal, a term which was used universally in the summer of 2020, has become, by early 2021, the normal way of life as one of the most important tools to protect ourselves in dealing with further waves of the Covid-19 infection.

This now not so new New Normal of social distancing and staying at home gave me an opportunity to start writing on something which seemed to be a worthwhile thing to do. But I am a novice, a somewhat idealistic novice, and even though I approached this writing with enthusiasm, I also viewed it with trepidation.

I am very mindful that in telling this story, I do not want it to be turned into a spark that initiates political arguments and debates about the rights and wrongs of the issues which are facing Hong Kong today. There is already too much of that in Hong Kong. Feeling deeply pained by the current problems, I developed an even more nostalgic feel for Hong Kong and what it has achieved over the past 60 years. This is my trip down memory lane and perhaps in taking the readers with me down this journey, some common ground can be found to initiate a process whereby the differences in the current Hong Kong society can be reconciled, a healing process can start and a new dawn begin.

By remembering the past, one can perhaps dare to glimpse into the future and in so doing, give everyone in Hong Kong a lift, a sense of optimism to rekindle the spirit of resourcefulness and enthusiasm which the people of Hong Kong are so famous for. The title of this book is therefore based on that premise.

Knowledge and views are best if they are honestly shared. So, I also hope that this non-academic narrative can serve as an enabler for the historians and social commentators to undertake more scholarly work in writing about Hong Kong. Maybe the little stories and anecdotes in this book can help them to get a feel of the spirit of Hong Kong, if ever such a personal perspective described here is thought to be worth their while to do so.

The people of Hong Kong in this book are the main reasons for the city's outstanding success. They are the producers, directors, writers and actors in this success story, both on the stage and off the stage. The script was written by them and therefore the credit should go entirely to them too. I hope that their renowned resilience and studiousness illustrated in this book will overcome whatever difficulties they may face and scale new heights for Hong Kong in the future. So, in many ways, I feel like a novice film critic, enthusiastic but with not too much nuance, after he has watched an award winning film and started to write a review of this film. Therefore, it would be entirely reasonable to assume that, for some observers, they may see my narrative in this book as being somewhat too sentimental and subjective, for which I offer no apology. Sentimentality, in some cases, is no bad thing, as it can humanize events, instead of cold, detached analysis. Without sentiments, success can be too detached, just like data on a spreadsheet.

Of course, there would be areas which I failed to address and the sentimentality, the critics may say, can compromise my objectivity over some issues. I have, however, endeavoured to try my best to address various issues by maintaining a degree of objectivity, balancing my love of Hong Kong with a writer's obligation to be impartial.

For these reasons, I have decided to use the starting point of this book to be when I was brought by my parents to Hong Kong in 1957 at the age of three. I have also organized the content in a somewhat chronological fashion, mirroring how I grew up with what I remembered. I do not necessarily feel that the readers need to agree with me. That is not the motive. Rather, I would find it personally gratifying if some readers can at least attain a certain degree of empathy with me when reading this book.

This book is intended to be apolitical, and hopefully, written as such. At the time of finishing this manuscript in March 2021, the world was full of uncertainties, often heated debates on global politics, even conspiracy theories were suggested, many of them wide of the mark, and none proven. These debates, perhaps too many of them, took place in the social media, the press, and even books have been published. This book, the readers can be reassured, stays away from any discussion of politics. The wise and incisive mind that one needs for a rational and informed discussion of the whats, the whys and the hows of the current state of global politics is simply beyond me.

One final reason for writing this book is that by sharing with the readers my own story and views of this very short story of Hong Kong, I hope to create for the readers a sense of my pride of Hong Kong and needless to say, give the readers in Hong Kong a sense of pride too.

CHAPTER 1
My Memories of Post-WW2 Hong Kong

An Unforgettable Book Cover

The first time I started to think about writing this book, the photo cover of a book surfaced in my mind. The name of the book was Hong Kong: Borrowed Place, Borrowed Time by Richard Hughes, published in 1968. Mr Hughes was an Australian journalist who spent much of his life in the Far East as a foreign correspondent for The London Times, The Economist and the Far Eastern Economic Review.

The cover was both striking and poignant. It was a photo covering a very iconic building of particular significance in Hong Kong, and that was the old Bank of China building. Right at the centre of the photo was the Bank of China with the Chinese national flag at the top and a big portrait of Chairman Mao Zedong in the front. One can tell that this photo was taken from the lawn of the Hong Kong Club, which was situated right in front of the bank. The photo also showed some Englishmen playing a very English sport called cricket o n a beautifully manicured lawn.

Back then, the Hong Kong Club was the ultimate symbol of British colonial privileges and elitism. The colonialists were playing a sport that absolutely none of the locals could understand nor had the inclination whatsoever to feel remotely interested in. It was an exclusive club, occupying a prime site, serving only the privileged British who came to work in Hong Kong as expatriates. No Chinese members were allowed, and the only Chinese who were inside, I would guess, were the servants and staff who worked there to serve the British. There were no non-white members.

Furthermore, if this photo could be expanded to cover a wider angle, it would have shown that next to the Bank of China would be the Hongkong and Shanghai Banking Corporation (HSBC), known by the locals as the Hong Kong Bank, which indeed it was, as its banking licence was issued by the Hong Kong government with the special permission to issue the Hong Kong dollar notes. And to the left of the photo, there would be the Hilton Hotel, which was one of the top two hotels in Hong Kong at the time (the other being the Peninsula Hotel in Kowloon). Next to the hotel would be Garden Road, stretching uphill and would lead to the American Consulate barely 500 metres away, passing St John's Cathedral. Behind these would be the Government House, where the governor of Hong Kong worked and resided.

This book's title and cover photo just about perfectly and accurately summed up the situation in Hong Kong in those early post- WW2 years. With one photo, it captured that essence of Hong Kong as a city – that its political and economic fate was inexorably tied with the UK, China, and the USA. While the USA might be a key player wielding enormous influence behind the scene, it was the UK and China which outwardly controlled the fate of Hong Kong. Most interestingly, the Supreme Court of Hong Kong, not included in the photo, was right in front of the Hong Kong Bank. This photo and its surroundings summed up Hong Kong for what it was.

Why have I come to know the locations of these buildings so well and with such clarity? There is a reason.

My Daily Walk

I gained admission to my secondary school in 1966 through a competitive secondary school entrance examination conducted by the Education Department of the Hong Kong government. Only those with high marks were allowed their first choice of a secondary school. I was lucky indeed and got selected to be admitted, as my first choice, to St Paul's Co-Educational College. This school is still there and widely acclaimed, even to this day, as one of the best schools in Hong Kong. There I met and made many lifelong good friends.

This school is situated in the mid-level area (this generally refers to the areas in Hong Kong halfway up Victoria Peak) on MacDonnell Road. At the time, there was no cross- harbour tunnel and there were only cross- harbour ferry services, of which the most famous was the Star Ferry. It is still running to date, and is now regarded by almost all as a truly iconic symbol of Hong Kong. At that time, I was living in Kowloon Peninsula, and it took me about 75 minutes every day to get to school by taking the ferry and then the bus. However, after school, I always walked to the Star Ferry with my schoolmates, as some of them also lived on the Kowloon side.

So for seven years, I walked down Garden Road every school day, and in so doing passed the American Consulate, St John's Cathedral, the Bank of China, the HSBC, the Supreme Court, Statue Square, the City Hall and City Hall Library to get to the Star Ferry. The Government House was just round the corner from the American Consulate, with blocks of main government office buildings across the road. Next to my own school was the all-boys St Joseph's College. No other school in the whole of Hong Kong was in such a location as special as these two schools in terms of their proximity to the centre of politics and power of Hong Kong.

It was a very pleasant walk, easy enough for a teenager, but it was only much later that I realized how incomparably significant it was to walk past these buildings nearly every day. This walk took only 20 minutes in total and could best be described as representing, without exaggeration, a real-life snapshot of the real institutions of power, influence and affluence in the history of Hong Kong.

These days, if I were to recommend a visitor to Hong Kong to take a short walk, I would suggest that he or she should start from the Peak Tram lower terminus on Garden Road and walk downhill along the road. I would point and explain meticulously to the visitor these iconic buildings along the way. No modern museum display, whatever the advanced technology used, can rival the real-life experience in the significance of this walk. And, if truth be told, the significance is still there to this day. Faded glory? No, after nearly 60 years, the significance is still there, perhaps even more so!

Given the chance, I would be happy to do the walk again for no reason other than nostalgia. Some cynics would argue that nostalgia in writing may run the risk of being an oversimplification of facts. These buildings, which are still very much in existence today, can tell their own stories without any simplification or elaboration. After all these years, only two buildings have changed in appearance, but not their significance. These changes, again, are very symbolic of Hong Kong in its short post- WW2 history. One change is the world-famous bamboo-like new Bank of China (BOC) Tower, whose address is actually 1 Garden Road, built in 1990 and designed by the internationally famous architect I.M. Pei, who also designed the Louvre Museum in Paris. The other is the very futuristic looking new Hongkong and Shanghai Banking Corporation (HSBC) Building, whose address is 1 Queen's Road Central, re-built in 1985 and designed by the equally famous Norman Foster. These two buildings are located less than 100 metres from each other. Hilton Hotel is no longer there and in its place stands one of the top commercial high-rise buildings belonging to a top local conglomerate owned and run by the richest tycoon in the history of Hong Kong.

Many postcards or google photos have been used, with great effect, to describe Hong Kong. Nearly all who look at these postcards and photos are impressed by the sheer beauties of modernity of Hong Kong, its glittering lights at night, architecturally designed high-rise buildings on both sides of Victoria Harbour, with the Lion Rock in the north at the background. The word iconic is often used to describe these postcards, but for me, the one really iconic image is the one I walked past every day for seven years.

The Timeframe

Nostalgia is what it is, and the very characteristic of nostalgia is that in addition to refreshing one's memories, it also compels one to focus the mind on things little remembered and long gone past. So, with these nostalgic memories to help and motivate me, I can begin to recollect and start reminiscing about various events to describe the recent past of Hong Kong. This I shall do so by grouping events into three periods, each representing a generation.

1. Between 1950 and 1980. 1980 was chosen as it was a watershed year when China began its Reform and Opening-Up policy. This I would call the Formative Years – the Era of Assimilation of the Immigrants.

2. Between 1980 and 1997. This represented the years before the return of sovereignty of Hong Kong back to China on July 1, 1997. This I would call the Era of Coming of Age.

3. Between 1997 and 2020. This was the period after Hong Kong returned to China under the One Country, Two Systems principle. This I would call the Emergence of Hong Kong as an International Financial Centre.

To understand the Hong Kong of today, it is important to at least be aware of the key events in the three periods which I outlined above. The events in these periods were pivotal in shaping developments in Hong Kong. Some events even shook Hong Kong. Moreover, these periods were chosen also to reflect on the impact on Hong Kong by the rapidly changing political, social and economic landscapes in China. It is not only necessary, but even mandatory in my view, that developments in Hong Kong could only be assessed and analysed by knowing and understanding the situations in China. This is equally important, for both the public sector, which has to undertake major infrastructure projects such as airport expansion and cross- harbour transport networks by road, rail or sea, and the private sector, which is responsible for just about everything else involving financial investment, business development and commercial activities. For both the public and private sectors, it would be foolhardy to make any major long-term decision in Hong Kong without factoring in the views and positions of the central government in Beijing.

In short, Hong Kong has to keep its fingers on the pulse by keeping note of events in China. Though history tells us that Hong Kong was in its creation a British colony right on the doorstep of China, one can hardly dispute the fact that Hong Kong has always been part of China, despite the colonial past of about 150 years. Hong Kong simply cannot survive without the blessing and the goodwill of Beijing.

Each of the periods outlined above has its generational impact too. These three periods would also demonstrate the transformative processes during which Hong Kong developed from being a small trading port, colonized by the UK in southern China, to becoming a famous international city and one of the global financial centres it is now today. The place and the geography have not changed, but the people have changed, or rather, have adapted to life in Hong Kong, a process which went exceptionally well against all expectations. Consequently, the economy powered ahead, governance improved and, more importantly, Hong Kong has in the meantime acquired its own local popular culture with its own way of life. The emergence of this unique brand of Hong Kong popular culture is a direct result of the cultural fusion between the East and the West, which will be explored further in Chapter 5.

Thus, I would put forward the view that Hong Kong is the first ever fusion city in the modern world. It has always been a fusion city even before the word fusion became fashionable. Fusion is very much part of the DNA makeup of the city. Any person who comes and lives here for a number of years will learn and almost certainly find the fusion of Western culture and Chinese culture very endearing and invigorating, unrivalled by anywhere else in the world. I went abroad for a long period of time and have learned and adapted to the Western culture, but I have not quite experienced the uniqueness of life in a fusion culture. And when a person like me goes back to Hong Kong, there would be the feeling, once again, unavoidably, of appreciation for this refreshing fusion culture.

CHAPTER 2
1950 to 1980: The Formative Years

The Immigrants

This period would be the decades of immigration from mainland China and was also the decades of hardship, of endurance, and of laying the foundation of the model of small government and free market enterprises. The combination of all these in the early years successfully indoctrinated into the mindset of the Hong Kong people a lifelong discipline of self-reliance, resilience and adaptability. The sowing of the seeds for future successes of Hong Kong was done in these early years. The culture of entitlement, in which the concept of safety net provision is obligated by the state and so commonly practised in the post- WW2 West, never really took hold in Hong Kong.

In 1949, the People's Republic of China was formed after the declaration by Chairman Mao Zedong in Tiananmen Square on October 1. This was the start of modern China as a republic, run by the Chinese Communist Party (CCP), after years of turmoil and devastation since the Manchu imperial rule was overthrown in 1911.

China was very poor then, because it had to, in its long struggle to maintain territorial integrity, endure both the Japanese invasion since 1937 (military aggression from Japan against China started even years before then in the northeast of China) and civil wars among the warlords prior to the Japanese invasion. So for a period of nearly 40 years, from 1911, China was war- torn. Finally, the CCP defeated the Nationalists of Kuomintang, led by Generalissimo Chiang Kai-shek, who then fled to Taiwan in 1949 and set up another administration.

Hong Kong was then regarded by many people in China as a small city with opportunities and a city that was governed by the British. So it was seen as the nearest foreign land right at the doorstep of southern China. Though it was a city that was controlled and run by the British through an appointed governor, the vast majority of the local inhabitants were ethnic Chinese who spoke the dialects prevalent in southern China. The Japanese Imperial Army, which occupied Hong Kong during WW2, was defeated after the dropping of atomic bombs, and left in 1945. For mainlanders, unlike emigrating to other countries like the USA or the UK, moving to Hong Kong was thought to be relatively easy and convenient as it involved only land travel.

There were then two types of immigrants to Hong Kong: those with entry visas granted by the Hong Kong government and those undocumented migrants without an entry visa. I was very fortunate as my parents managed to get us all to Hong Kong through properly granted visas. For those undocumented migrants without an entry visa, they often risked their lives by attempting to cross the borders by either climbing and crossing mountains, or travelling in illegal small boats in the dark to evade detection by Chinese gunboats which patrolled the seas along the southern coast. Some even swam across the border from some obscured and unguarded starting points in China to various points in the small islands around Hong Kong, and this swimming journey could stretch up to eight kilometres.

There were, from the 1950s to the 1960s, hundreds of thousands of immigrants from China. There were no accurate figures but in the 1950s, it was estimated that up to 100,000 people per month arrived in Hong Kong from China.

Thus, dealing with immigrants from China had always been one of the major policy challenges for the Hong Kong government in this period. Hong Kong simply at the time did not have the infrastructure or the necessary amenities to deal with these arrivals. To put it bluntly, the government was simply too overwhelmed, ill-equipped and ill-prepared to provide basic needs such as housing, medical services or social services. There were no concrete plans to settle the regular waves of arrivals, legal or otherwise. For many of the undocumented migrants, they often, in those days, lived in squalid conditions of wooden huts up by the mountains with poor sanitation, and no water or power supply.

Yet, these immigrants, legal or illegal, all came with one single and determined desire. They came to make a living and in so doing, a better life. Most of these immigrants were rapidly absorbed into some sort of job to make a basic living. There was no legislation for employment protection at the time. There were no statutory holidays, minimum wages or medical covers. And yet, for these brave immigrants, unleashed into the labour market in post- WW2 Hong Kong, all had the extraordinary mindset of willingness to take any jobs on offer, however poorly paid they might be, rather than waiting for handouts. When I reflected on these from the comforts in the later years of my life, I cannot help but question my own inadequacy to truly appreciate what these previous generations went through all those years ago. These stories need to be told, and retold again.

Originally the predominant dialects spoken by the indigenous population in Hong Kong were Cantonese, Chiu Chow and Hakka; the latter two groups were people whose origins were from the coastal areas of the vast province of Guangdong. The Hakka people were mainly fishermen, living in boats or sampans as they were locally called, around the islands and the coastal areas of Hong Kong. Their younger ones often went ashore in search of hard, manual and unskilled labour work. They, just like the other group called the Chiu Chow people, were industrious, resilient and clannish.

The other distinct set of immigrants were the northern Chinese, mainly from Shanghai, which is the city of my birth. They spoke a different dialect. Shanghai was at the time the most modern city in China. Many Shanghainese, as they are called, were skilled in business and commerce, well versed in sophisticated trading and manufacturing know-how. And when many of these Shanghainese came to Hong Kong, they brought with them capital and a drive for investments and start-ups, especially in setting up factories for manufacturing. Soon they started a thriving manufacturing industry in Hong Kong, especially in the textiles sector, providing further structured (regular hours and salaries) employment opportunities. That was how some people in Hong Kong started to make a living, by becoming factory workers. Other not so lucky ones, short of the opportunities of factory employments, earned a meagre living by providing hard and cheap labour, often working for more than 18 hours a day with no breaks or a day off. This usually involved extremely labour intensive, repetitive and monotonous manual jobs such as making plastic flowers or wigs by assembling the parts by hands. There was only minimal industrial automation in those years. Meanwhile, the more innovative ones chose to set up primitive food stalls selling locally made snacks at incredibly cheap prices. So, by different means, these immigrants started to make a living. They all showed great fortitude and perseverance, all playing a part in initiating the future success of Hong Kong. Their spirits of hard work and of endurance all helped to generate an indelible community spirit of enterprise and entrepreneurship. This was how Hong Kong started in those early years.

Housing and Social Challenges

Living conditions could be very hard for the majority of the migrants, especially the undocumented ones. Their shady living quarters were full of hazards. They ran the risk of their homes being destroyed by fire when a fuse was overloaded, or landslides during periods of heavy rain. Often people were made homeless as a result of these disasters. The overcrowding and poor sanitation conditions also led to infective outbreaks like cholera, typhoid fever and tuberculosis.

I still remember, when I was a child, being told about a huge fire in an area called Shek Kip Mei, which at one stroke made 53,000 people homeless on December 25, 1953. It was after this that the then governor of Hong Kong, Sir Alexander Graham, started to build resettlement estates of multi-storey buildings with shared kitchens and sanitary facilities to house the homeless. That was the early and the first post- WW2 initiative to find a solution to a perpetual problem in Hong Kong – the housing needs of an ever increasing population.

These multi-storey buildings were small dwellings with barely any living space but did serve their purpose at the time – to put a concrete roof above people's heads. Though not acceptable by modern standards, it was nevertheless a make- do arrangement and was at least safer than wooden huts. In fact, if one looks around Hong Kong now, none of these buildings exist any more. These buildings were history, but for me, the precious memories of these multi-storey buildings are deep in my mind. They told me much more about these newly arrived immigrants (I myself was lucky, looking back, as my parents were at least able to rent a flat for us to live in), what they did and how they lived. I can still remember, to this very day, that when I was about 11 years old, I went on a visit to my primary school classmate who lived with his parents in one of these multi-storey make-do buildings. The few times I went there, we played table tennis in the open communal areas. There was childhood happiness. Everyone was content that there was a roof above our heads. There was no bitterness or resentment.

To understand the scale and the reason for these waves of immigration into Hong Kong, one needs to be aware of the situation in China, where there were regular and massive political movements and ideological campaigns. There was the Great Leap Forward in the late 1950s which led to famine and starvation, then the failed economic model of the People's Commune, and the political upheavals of the Cultural Revolution which lasted from 1966 to 1976. These political movements were actually huge social experiments aimed at achieving a utopian state of society through massive state sponsored political campaigns, but it proved to have the opposite effect. The strife for ideological purity led to untold hardships affecting the lives of millions. Therefore, some mainland Chinese saw Hong Kong as a natural escape route, perhaps the only escape route, away from fear of regular ideological purges and also the need of fulfilling the basic human desire to banish hunger.

For many of these immigrants to Hong Kong, especially among the undocumented ones, often they did not have access to basic healthcare needs, nor educational provision for the young. Even water supply had to be rationed, at about several hours a day, from a public tap to be shared with many. Infectious diseases such as cholera, typhoid and tuberculosis were often rampant. There was no social protection or provision of a safety net of any scale. It was, sadly, a case of live and let live. Yet these people gritted their teeth with a stoical endurance for which I have nothing but the highest admiration.

One of the reasons that they were able to bear this hardship was that, for once, they could have a choice on what work to apply for without having their chance of application for work assessed, and indeed assigned, by the state, on the basis of their ideological background and political purity. To them, despite the low pay or long working hours, at least they could start to earn a living on their own freewill and choice. As it turned out, they proved to be diligent and studious. Their rationale was simple and unsophisticated. Any earned payment was better than no payment. They would not expect a government handout as there was no government handout. The practice of the post- WW2 social welfare safety net, as started by the West, was simply non-existent in this tiny British colony.

Over time, their sheer endurance and ability to work hard gradually paid off. They helped to lay the foundation for the success of Hong Kong in the ensuing years. They were the essential, unmatchable and indispensable parts of the fabrics of Hong Kong which all gelled together to propel the local economy forward. Many of them pooled their hard earned money to start small businesses. They were never idle. Life for them was just work, work and work. This endurance of hardship and entrepreneurial spirit prepared them well for what life held in store for them. Work ethics are words often used by Western commentators to describe the common Chinese cultural trait, and this was demonstrated so unambiguously and distinctively by the people of Hong Kong in those early years.

The Unrest

However, there was some political unrest too, as there were some Nationalist sympathizers, who, instead of moving to Taiwan, chose to come to Hong Kong. On October 10, 1956, there was a political clash between the Nationalist and the Communist sympathizers. It was called the October unrest, and the trigger was the hanging and display of the different national flags as the People's Republic of China celebrated its National Day on October 1, while the Nationalists in Taiwan celebrated their National Day on October 10. The unrest was quickly quelled by the Hong Kong Police, since the riots did not have widespread public support. But the seeds were then sown that Hong Kong would always be in a politically sensitive position, caught between the two rival factions. The colonial Hong Kong government had to handle any future delicate issues of such nature with sensitivity and nuance. A political section called the Special Branch in the Police Force was then set up to deal with sensitive political issues.

Another major political event in Hong Kong was the Communist inspired riots in 1967, triggered this time by a labour dispute in a factory which made plastic flowers. Special mention here must be made that prior to the 1967 riots in Hong Kong, a similar riot also occurred in Macau, which was a city first settled by the Portuguese way back in 1557, during the imperial Ming Dynasty in China and later ceded to Portugal in 1887 under the Sino-Portuguese Treaty of Peking. Macau is a neighbouring city to Hong Kong, about 65 kilometres away, separated by the South China Sea.

The Macau riot occurred on December 3, 1966 which happened against a background of the feverish Cultural Revolution in China. It was in direct response by the public in Macau to a violent police crackdown on Chinese protestors demonstrating against corruption and colonialism in Macau. There were massive labour strikes which paralysed Macau. Pressured by business leaders in Macau and the mainland Chinese government in Beijing, the colonial Portuguese government agreed to meet the demands of the strikers and apologized for the police crackdown.

This complete success of the strikers in Macau and its quick resolution undoubtedly had a significant galvanizing effect on the Hong Kong riots. The labour dispute in the plastic flower factory quickly got out of control. The riots spread rapidly to the rest of Hong Kong. They then became politically supported and organized also by the local pro-communist faction, spurred on by the feverish Cultural Revolution sentiments in China and the recent success in Macau, where the Portuguese colonial government quickly capitulated.

The Hong Kong riots led to an open and often violent confrontation between the police and the rioters. The Hong Kong government had to declare curfews to control the situation. There were strikes organized by the unions, as well as street demonstrations and home-made street bombs disrupting civic order. There were even border clashes with fatalities, and the fear was that the People's Liberation Army (PLA) from China would march south across the border to take over Hong Kong as the local British army garrison would simply be outnumbered to repel or resist any military advances from China.

The situation became very tense and precarious. Things were reaching boiling point. It was thought by some that the colonial government in Hong Kong was losing control, and it was widely rumoured that the British government back in London was actively contemplating withdrawing from Hong Kong, and the appropriate signals were sent from London to Beijing. At this crucial moment, cool heads from China prevailed. The urbane elderly and stately Premier Zhou Enlai, who was close to Chairman Mao and whose experience in foreign affairs was second to none, obtained the support of Chairman Mao and issued direct orders from Beijing to the local communists in Hong Kong to stop the rioting.

China, in its grand strategic vision, had no intention of taking over Hong Kong at that point. It saw Hong Kong as having the strategic importance in offering significant national, political and economic interest to China, serving as a window to the West. In retrospect, this was a truly knife-edge moment for Hong Kong in the past 60 years and at the eleventh hour, the Chinese leadership decided that the status quo needed to be preserved. Taking back control and governance of Hong Kong could be left to a later stage, in accordance with the terms of the Second Convention of Peking signed in 1898 which stated that the New Territories lease would expire in 1997.

The Post-1967 Road to Prosperity

From then onwards, having just gone through the 1967 riots, the status of Hong Kong was assured and political uncertainty was temporarily put aside, Hong Kong was truly able to start its legendary economic boom, to the envy of the world. This boom was a combination of the Hong Kong government's principal economic policy of small government with a non-interventional tariff-free market approach to its economy and enterprises. This enabled businesses to develop and prosper while the government concentrated on investing in education, infrastructure, housing and medical services.

The second university in Hong Kong, called the Chinese University of Hong Kong, was already set up in 1963 (the first university in Hong Kong called the University of Hong Kong was set up way back in 1911). The two universities were instrumental in providing the key education and training in various fields needed for Hong Kong.

Over the subsequent years, the fruits of success of economic progress and the rapid pace of the modernization of Hong Kong led to the emergence of a thriving middle class with skilled professionals such as accountants, managers, administrators, lawyers, doctors, bankers, teachers and university academics. This emergence of the middle class all contributed, together with the success and prosperity in the business sector, to success in transforming Hong Kong to become a more open, liberal and civic society.

The Emergence of the Middle Class and the Elitists

Gradually, through the openness of Hong Kong as a British colony and free access to skill sets and ideas from the West, many of the new middle class were able to polish their professional skills and reach international standards in various fields. Many of these young professionals were trained and educated in the West. The pool of experience they accrued in areas such as accounting, financing, stock trading, banking, and land surveying all helped to prepare Hong Kong to achieve the realization of its aspirations of being one of the leading financial centres in the world. Many of these professionals not only were very successful but became household names as well. Some were public spirited and were drafted in by the governor of

Hong Kong to serve as members of the Executive Council. This council functioned much like an inner cabinet which offered advice to the governor through the width and depth of the collective expertise that these members possessed. Thus the government was able to tap into their professional and business know-how in formulating its policies. This system had served Hong Kong well.

Over the years, this system inadvertently produced a group of well-to-do, well-connected people that were regarded as the elites of Hong Kong. These elites were often also members of exclusive private clubs in Hong Kong such as the Country Club or Jockey Club.

There was this joke and not without a grain of truth, that there were four ruling bodies (unofficially known as the Big Four) in Hong Kong. They were, in descending order: the Royal Hong Kong Jockey Club (the word Royal was removed after 1997), HSBC, Jardine Matheson Trading House (which prospered initially on the opium trade in China in the 19th Century, and which moved its domicile prior to 1997), and finally the Hong Kong government. This Big Four were firmly headed and controlled by the British, though the local able Chinese were allowed to rise through the ranks. The elites in Hong Kong were therefore, directly or indirectly, connected to the Big Four and had in turn benefited from the personal or professional connections through the Big Four. Major policies could not be decided without the blessings of this Big Four. Some even said that important policy initiatives were often mooted and sounded off in the director boxes at the Royal Hong Kong Jockey Club on racing days on a Saturday afternoon, where the senior directors of these big companies were almost, by the power of the positions they held in the companies, also directors of this racing club. Such was the unique privilege that the Royal Hong Kong Jockey Club had, that not only was it the only institution in Hong Kong with a government issued betting licence, it also had the unique Royal Charter, granted by Her Majesty the Queen in the UK, as the club was a non-profit making, professionally run charitable organization.

The position of the Royal Hong Kong Jockey Club and the importance of the Club in the minds of the people of Hong Kong was immortalized by the famous words spoken by the most senior official sent from Beijing to Hong Kong in the 1980s. In his liaison work between Beijing and Hong Kong, he used a metaphor, with great effect, to reassure the Hong Kong public at the time of the Sino-British negotiations on the future of Hong Kong by saying: 'Horse racing will carry on as usual, and so will dancing' in Hong Kong after 1997. Now, dancing of course could happen in any private parties or dance halls, and in China, but horse racing is unique to Hong Kong, China does not allow betting or horse racing. The implication of course was that the people of Hong Kong should have no worries, as life in Hong Kong would be much the same after 1997. More will be written about the Jockey Club in a later chapter.

In the history of the emergence of elitism and an elite class in Hong Kong, none can be better exemplified by Sir Ho Tung and his descendants. His was by far the first one off the block, even before WW2. His name was Robert Ho Tung, twice knighted, in 1915 and then 1955. He was simply known locally as Sir Ho Tung, or the grand old man of Hong Kong. Ho was a smart Chinese businessman who had some Jewish heritage in him. He acted as a buyer for the aforementioned Jardine Matheson Trading House. In those days, due to the policy on import of goods imposed by the late Qing Dynasty, every good that was imported into or exported from Hong Kong had to be dealt through a designated buyer approved by the Qing government. He was one of them, working for Jardine Matheson trading house (trading house was known by the local Chinese as 'Hong' in Cantonese), including opium in the early days. Jardine Matheson, being a British company and Hong, had to rely on him for his local expertise to advise on its trade and to decide on what to buy and what to sell. Mr Ho held such a position in the company. He was a genius and a true Hong Kong native. He amassed a fortune which served his descendants well for decades. He was truly the first generation well-connected elitist. Many of his descendants also became part of the elite establishment and became outstanding professionals, academics or businessmen. Mr Ho was also a major philanthropist, his charity work left its footprints all over Hong Kong and some even in Macau.

Many other first generations of the super-rich families in Hong Kong were also like Mr Ho in their philanthropist work. The Kadoories, who were Iraqi Jews immigrated from Shanghai to Hong Kong, became a household name by investing in hotels and utilities such as electricity in Hong Kong. Their business acumen was equally matched by their enthusiasm in undertaking charity work in the community. They helped to fund and develop the successful farming charity for the growth of organic food in the New Territories. Other families, such as the Tangs, the Foks, the Fungs, the Lis and the Kwoks all did the same. Their vast wealth was the enabler for their philanthropy work. The motto of 'taketh from society, giveth to society' runs deep in these families.

Furthermore, these rich and successful people were seen by the poor as entrepreneurs and became role models. There was no resentment of their wealth. Their business skills were admired and their modus operandi was often copied. In short, their success story served as a road map which the poor would aspire to and learn from. The presence of such an elite and rich group, all occupying positions of influence in the affairs and running of Hong Kong, did not lead to antipathy by the poor. Quite the opposite: it made the poor wish to be like them. This was all the more surprising as the world then was a bipolar world when the Cold War essentially split the world into two ideological blocs. Communism, which preaches the importance of the proletariat class, was aiming to topple capitalism. Yet, Hong Kong, right at the southern border of China, the world's largest communist country, was able and allowed to practise capitalism unabated and even made such an extraordinary success out of it. In those years of economic boom in Hong Kong, there was no clash of ideologies, notwithstanding the 1967 riots, and there was no obsession among the public with isms, be it socialism, communism or capitalism. There was this single and unifying belief and determination to turn Hong Kong into a successful modern city, free of ideological clashes or constraints. Of course, there were the left wing and right wing press or publications, but that never led to any grievances or clashes. It was truly a society with freedom of press and expression. Divergence of opinions was respected, different views were tolerated and debated, but never condemned with venom.

This phenomenon of not resenting but aspiring to the rich, together with the tolerance of various views, was truly one of the real hallmarks of life in Hong Kong. But regrettably, this was not too much written about in the West.

The reason for this phenomenon of not resenting the rich, but rather admiring the rich, is hard to explain in any sociological terms, though it can be explained in free market terms, in the sense that personal gain (legal of course) is quite possibly the best motivator of all. It also reflected a certain degree of maturity and pragmatism by the people of Hong Kong in a situation where they found themselves making a capitalistic living in a colony right on the doorstep of China. In addition, the proximity of Hong Kong to China enabled Hong Kong to be very well informed about what was happening in China. Some Hong Kong people actually had personal experiences or knew of friends and relatives who had lived through the difficulties and turbulences that China had gone through. So, in their pursuit for a better living, there was no grandstanding as the people of Hong Kong were acutely sensitive of the feelings of their compatriots in China. They felt lucky to be in a society like Hong Kong, free to pursue what they liked to pursue. They were energized by the liberating environment. Here, everyone could have a chance to share the formula of riches and make a success of life. There was no intellectual property associated with this formula; everyone could have a go. Over the years, it all added up to making Hong Kong an internationally famous and admired city.

The Eradication of Corruption

But life is never just roses, milk and honey. Up to the 1970s, there were some real social problems besetting Hong Kong. For the ordinary and the poor people who wanted to make a living, corruption was not only rife but was part of life too. Hard cash, which was very often hard earned, was needed always to grease the wheels of services.

The small street vendors trying to make a living without a licence to trade could not ply their trade unless cash was first passed from their hands to the hands of the police, who patrolled the streets. Once cash had changed hands, the police would turn a blind eye to their unlicensed trade.

This institutional corruption was particularly prevalent in the running of vice activities organized by the triads, the name given to organized crime in Hong Kong. The vice here included illegal gambling, drug dealings, extortion and prostitution. Other public and essential services also, to various extents, partook in these cash for services. Firemen would not operate their hose till cash was exchanged, and even for a poor patient lying in bed in a scarcely functional public hospital, he or she might have to pass some cash to the staff to get things done, or their care would be secondary to those who did pay! There were horror stories but nonetheless true. This form of cash-only corruption was also prevalent in business transactions, and these were called kickbacks.

This rife corruption, begrudgingly tolerated by the public, offered an uncomfortable and unpalatable facet of life in Hong Kong in those days.

Then came the scandal of Peter Godber, a Deputy District Commander of the Royal Hong Kong Police Force (the word Royal was dropped after the handover in 1997). Godber was an expatriate police officer recruited from the UK. At the time, everyone knew the police were corrupt. It was widely known that they were paid in hard cash by the triads to turn a blind eye to the running of illegal gambling dens, heroin and drug smuggling, and brothels. The occasional arrests were only for show and demonstrative purposes. Only small flies were caught. Such corruption was hard to stamp out because it was all very well coordinated, syndicated and even accepted by some as part of the necessity of life! In other words, this widespread institutional corruption, especially among the police force, was a shameful aspect of the Hong Kong way of life. The victims were almost always from the more vulnerable section of society.

Peter Godber had a warrant for his arrest issued by the Hong Kong government in 1973 for being one of the leaders of the corruption gangs in the police force. But he managed to avoid arrest by absconding to London. It sent shock waves to London and caused an uproar in London and Hong Kong. He was then arrested in London and extradited to Hong Kong for a high profile trial which was the first for a British government law enforcement officer. He was found guilty and imprisoned for four years. His high profile trials sent a clear signal to the other police officers who were involved in corruption. Some accomplices in the police force, especially those of Chinese ethnicity, escaped to Taiwan or Canada before charges could be brought against them.

This was a shameful chapter. The government had no choice but to do something to weed out at a stroke the widespread corruption which would cause immense reputational damage to Hong Kong as an international city of commerce and trading or its image would be forever tarnished.

Sir Murray MacLehose was then the governor of Hong Kong, and he was determined to root out this shameful practice as a result of the Peter Godber scandal. He set up the Independent Commission Against Corruption (ICAC) in 1974. This was a master stroke and the setting up of this commission was one of the major post-war landmark successes in Hong Kong.

One of the clauses in the charge of corruption was ingenious and that was 'income not commensurate with assets'. The ICAC was given sweeping powers granted by the governor to investigate the wealth of any suspected individual, both in the private and public sectors.

The ICAC proved to be highly effective in stamping out corruption. Furthermore, the ICAC decided that the best way of dealing with corruption was to prevent corruption, so it also initiated a massive and extremely effective public information and education campaign against corruption. The ICAC was feared by some, i.e. those who were corrupt, but was widely supported by the public. Over time, the ICAC successfully helped to transform the image of the public services of Hong Kong, especially the police force, making it one of the most efficient and incorruptible of the public services in the eyes of the world.

In addition to the setting up of the ICAC, the Hong Kong government also actively started a comprehensive programme of succession planning. A long-term strategy was put in place whereby senior civil service positions were to be filled by well-trained local Chinese, often with a period of sabbatical in the UK. Expatriates from the UK were no longer parachuted in to fill senior government positions.

Prior to this new policy of mandating and training the locals for higher office, only the rank and file members of the civil service were filled by local Chinese. Nearly all senior government officials were expatriates appointed in London. Most were bureaucrats in their professional background who came to take up senior positions in the colony with little experience of China or Hong Kong. Their lack of understanding and appreciation of the local culture in an increasingly complex society created a real barrier for the making and execution of policy.

This policy of grooming homegrown talents who were familiar with Hong Kong to take up senior positions in the Hong Kong government was a success. However, it should also be mentioned that there were some very able and well-respected expatriates who came to Hong Kong, and not a few of them stayed in Hong Kong for quite a long time. They carved out a distinguished career in Hong Kong. A classic illustration to this was Sir Jack Cater, who did have extensive experience working both initially in the public and latterly in the private sector in Hong Kong. He was appointed as the first commissioner of the ICAC by the then governor of Hong Kong, and after retiring, he joined China Light & Power Company and became the head of Hong Kong Nuclear Investment Company, a nuclear power plant venture at Daya Bay in Guangdong province. The other was Sir David Akers-Jones. He was the Chief Secretary of Hong Kong from 1985 to 1987, and was briefly Acting Governor of Hong Kong.

As a result of this policy of succession, all those who worked above a certain rank in various government departments started to have a chance of being sent abroad for further studies or training, mainly to distinguished institutions in the UK, thus enabling them to learn the machines of government and to climb up their career ladder. Over time, a group of well-trained, talented and experienced civil service officials was formed, ready to take over the reins and run Hong Kong when the British handed over the territory back to China. In fact, at the time of the handover, nearly all top governments officials were local Chinese who had been trained and had worked in Hong Kong for years.

Promotion of Recreational Amenities

The 1967 riots, as described previously, were mainly a politically motivated event. The riots, together with the widespread police corruption, reflected areas of weakness within the society. These left a deep scar both on the people and the Hong Kong government, despite the continued economic boom and increasing prosperity. There was a need to review what other major changes were needed in the way Hong Kong was run.

One of the key measures that was introduced in Hong Kong after the trauma of the riots was to address the problem that leisure and recreational facilities for the people, especially the young, were grossly inadequate, in fact, even non-existent. The main pastimes of the local people were either the Chinese game of mahjong, gambling, horse racing, or listening to radios. Hong Kong did not have its own civic identity or its own culture.

So the government started the initiatives of organizing many community events to provide for more recreational activities. Venues for public entertainment were created. More public swimming pools and sporting facilities were built. Hiking paths (of which the most famous with global popularity was the MacLehose Trail, named after Governor MacLehose) were created in and around the countryside, with barbecue facilities as well. As a matter of fact, Hong Kong boasts one of the most scenic and easily accessible countrysides in the world. Local concerts or shows were regularly hosted. A new free-to-air, non-cable television studio was set up in 1967.

All these new initiatives were aimed to enrich the life of the hardworking people of Hong Kong by providing them with some leisure options and pleasures, be it indoors or outdoors. The ideas here were twofold. The main one was to give the public some choices of spending their free time, but equally important was to provide for the younger generation a chance to develop their creative talents, so they might have a wider career choice in areas like singing, performing, the media industry or even sport, especially football. Hong Kong in that period actually produced some of the finest footballers in Asia. More on the development of local culture will be discussed in Chapter 5.

The people of Hong Kong started to have a taste of a more variable but stable lifestyle as a result of these various initiatives. Life was beginning to offer them choices. Business confidence moved into the top gear and a unique Hong Kong way of life was starting to emerge. With all the various initiatives, it is my view that the main credit ought to go to Governor MacLehose. He was energetic and forward-thinking. His policies were well-received and remembered by the vast majority of the people of Hong Kong, with great fondness and affection.

Housing and Education Reforms

In 1972, one year after his arrival in Hong Kong, Governor MacLehose started a major infrastructure programme which was daring in its scope for the governor of this British colony. He announced and launched a ten-year housing policy to provide 'permanent self-contained accommodation in a reasonable environment' for the people of Hong Kong who could not afford to buy their own properties. This was groundbreaking both in its scale and its ambition. From then on, the government of Hong Kong was obliged to provide public low-cost housing for low-income families, with the hope that there would be no more homeless or squatters. This was a direct policy response to the social unrest in 1967, even though the trigger for the unrest was an industrial dispute which later turned out to be politically motivated. In addition, he also announced a nine-year compulsory education programme which meant a free primary school education for six years and junior high education for three years.

I was in senior high school then in Hong Kong, hoping to get into the University of Hong Kong, and I remembered very well that when I read about the announcement in the newspaper, I was very touched and felt somewhat shaken even, as up to 1972, we, the ordinary people of Hong Kong, could never have imagined something like that when housing and education were at the top of the government policy agenda. It was as if Governor MacLehose had, at a stroke, introduced us to a modern world where social benevolence for the vulnerable section of society was just as important as the success of the economy. I now realized, many years later, that one cannot do without the other. When I do think back about the state of my mind at that time, I cannot help having wet eyes for what he did in 1972.

Years later, when I arrived in the UK in 1980, I was able to debate with my British friends who often wound me up, very mischievously, by asking me: apart from money, what else were the people of Hong Kong interested in? I was able to debate with them, at length, without fail and with immense pride and rationality, backed up by facts, how civility and success were achieved in this faraway colony, acquired as a result of the infamous Opium War, endowed with no resources other than its people, and started its slow march to join the international league! So I told them, it had nothing to do with the pursuit of money for its own sake, but more to do with giving the freedom and opportunities for people to make a living and excel in their own life.

Initiation of Dialogue with Beijing

Governor MacLehose also knew that the long-term future of Hong Kong could only be resolved by engaging in discussion with China, so he went to see the paramount leader in China, Mr Deng Xiaoping, in 1979. This was necessary as the New Territories land lease from China would expire in 1997, so the real estate developers in Hong Kong needed to decide if investments in the New Territories were feasible. In their discussions, Deng reportedly said to MacLehose that China did intend to take back control of Hong Kong, but the investors could put their mind at ease. The implications clearly were that sovereignty must be returned to China, while the economic foundations which made Hong Kong such a success would continue. The 'One Country, Two Systems' principle had not been formulated at the time.

A few years prior to that, back in 1977, when Deng became the paramount leader and the Cultural Revolution had just passed, China was still bearing the scars of the upheavals. Deng then initiated a major groundbreaking policy called Reform and Opening Up (*gaige kaifang* in Putonghua) in 1979.

China, up to then, was a country which was very much closed to the outside world. Its economic model was primarily based on the Soviet model of central planning by the state. Deng explained, in the broadest of terms, that this reform and opening up (*gaike kaifang*) policy should be seen as China steering towards 'socialism with Chinese characteristics'. In other words, Deng wanted to open up China to the world, with an economic model based on the free market principle and not a centrally planned model, which was proven to be ineffective during the Soviet Union days when nearly all its member states followed the central planning model but saw their economy stagnating as a result, while the West was pulling ahead in its economic revival after WW2. This would ultimately lead to the collapse of the Soviet Union after the Berlin Wall came down in 1989.

When Governor MacLehose returned from his visit to Deng, it was very clear to him and to London that for Hong Kong to continue to develop and prosper, the next phase leading up to

1997 would be crucial. It was clear also that China was in no rush to take back Hong Kong and would only do so when the timing was right for China in a geopolitical sense. It was imperative that Hong Kong had to get its own house in order in terms of continued stability and prosperity. There was therefore a very clear need, at the highest levels of both governments, to start a process when the future governance of Hong Kong could be discussed, formulated and agreed. On this particular point, I think Governor MacLehose deserved some high marks for his achievements in getting the clear message on the real intentions of the Chinese leaders regarding the future of Hong Kong.

Governor MacLehose was one of the best governors who ever served in Hong Kong. He was also the longest serving governor from 1971-1982 and is still regarded by many of my generation with the fondest of memories and highest of praise.

I was once, many years ago, walking on a popular footpath on Victoria Peak under beautiful sunshine one Saturday evening in the autumn when I happened to bump into him. He was walking briskly on his own followed by a bodyguard in civilian clothes a few yards behind him. He even said hello to me. I formed the impression that he was a keen walker and a hiker. Shortly before he retired and left Hong Kong, the people of Hong Kong, as was the tradition, wished to say goodbye to a good leader by erecting some sort of permanent memorial statue or building for him, or naming a hospital after him. Yet, he chose to have a hiking path in the New Territories using his name, which was then called the MacLehose Trail. Such was the way the people held him with affection that this trail was opened in 1979, about three years before he retired. This is a 100-kilometre hiking trail criss-crossing the beautiful countryside in the New Territories, starting from Pak Tam Chung in Sai Kung in the east to Tuen Mun in the west. It remains to this day a very popular hiking path for both the local people and international tourists. This is a very fitting way of remembering a good man.

At this point, I would like to share a personal story in an effort to explain how such hard work and resilience, which are so ingrained in the people of Hong Kong, could, with vigour and determination, lead to success in those formative years.

When I was about 11, I used to go to buy my own breakfast from the street stalls. One such morning, I accidentally noticed that in a small alleyway there was a young couple, who had recently come to Hong Kong from the north of China, selling the sort of breakfast that a northern Chinese like me would love. These were hot soya milk, fried plain dough and sticky rice made into a rice ball with some fillings of pickled vegetables and minced pork.

All these snacks had to be freshly prepared, they could not be stored overnight as there was no fridge in the alleyway, and I guessed they could not have afforded to have one anyway. I was not sure either if they needed to pay any rent as it was very much a small part of an alleyway, with only a few passers-by. But for me, as a young child, I loved that breakfast! It was very cheap and very tasty. I could not quite talk to them as both were so busy preparing and selling the food, but I did figure out that they couldn't speak a word of Cantonese, which was the most common dialect used in Hong Kong.

I went there often, almost like a ritual every few mornings. After about a year, they were no longer in the alleyway, but were selling their snacks all day in a tiny corner shop a few steps from the end of the alleyway. They still worked hard but they looked happy. I went there often and started to talk to them. Their Cantonese was by then functional but with a heavy northern accent. One day, they told me they had saved enough and, assisted by a bank loan, they had bought the little shop to run their business at a proper place to sell authentic northern Chinese breakfast in the morning and then snacks like pork buns the rest of the day. I could tell the excitement on their face. One of them told me they had plans to have children who could be brought up in Hong Kong.

I never saw them again after I moved to the UK. The alleyway and the place where their shop was had now been converted to modern high-rise buildings. I have often thought about them and chances were, barring any unforeseen circumstances, they and their children are now truly settled, and happy too. I do hope so.

I am reminiscing with this personal story not because it is extraordinary, but because it is so ordinary. This is a story which was all too common in Hong Kong, a story of how the poor, no matter what the odds were against them, fought on, worked hard, and came good in the end. To me, this was a beautiful story as it is very much part of the Hong Kong story. For many, many of these poor legal and undocumented migrants braving for a new life, Hong Kong was a place of opportunity and hope for them. And since, like them, I was also an immigrant, I share with them this cherished feeling of gratitude and fulfilment.

CHAPTER 3

1980 to 1997: The Golden Years of an Extraordinary City of International Acclaim

These were the boom years, the years during which Hong Kong emerged and arrived at the international stage. There are many reasons why Hong Kong started to take off from the 1980s. Each of these reasons together reinforced each other, while acting synergistically to achieve success, overcoming difficulties and adversities along the way. The reasons for this remarkable achievement can be boiled down to several key factors for which I shall attempt to elaborate further here.

The China Factor

China, having just recovered from the Cultural Revolution, decided on a major national policy in 1979 of reform and opening up (*gaige kaifang*). This policy is essentially a groundbreaking economic reform by using a market- based economic model to drive up production and investment. It started off mainly in the agricultural sector by allowing the farmers to sell their extra production (after selling the target production to the state) in the private market, as an incentive to boost up their production and allowing private investments in the manufacturing sector with a view to selling well made but cheap consumer products for both the internal and export markets.

For the manufacturing sector, the Chinese government designated some special economic zones (SEZs) to pilot this policy. These zones were geographically located near the coastal areas. Among these, one of them was a city called Shenzhen, which is just at the border from Hong Kong. Shenzhen at the time was a little known fishing village with a local population of only around 60,000.

These special economic zones provided cheap land plus young and willing workers (known as migrant workers who moved there from other parts of China in search of work) as the basis to attract foreign direct investment. There were tax advantages too. All combined to create a modern business-friendly and investment-friendly environment. This provided a golden opportunity for Hong Kong as it was already felt that, by the early 1980s, the room for further expansion in the local manufacturing industry was very limited. Land prices in Hong Kong were then already prohibitively expensive for factory production.

This reform and opening up initiative in China was welcomed by the modern and smart entrepreneurs in Hong Kong. They saw it as a perfect opportunity and tailor-made solution for further expansion of their business. It could not have happened at a better time for Hong Kong. The whole industrial sector, especially those involving factories and manufacturing, started to invest significantly in China, particularly in Shenzhen and its neighbouring area called Dongguan, because of logistical advantage due to their proximity to Hong Kong. This was a win-win situation which proved to be extraordinarily successful. These investments have continued up to the present day. According to the English language newspaper Global Times published in China, in 2019, nearly 80% of new foreign investment projects in the city of Shenzhen received funding from Hong Kong. Elsewhere, foreign direct investments from Japan, the USA, Taiwan and Germany also started to pour into China, all helping to propel China into what is now known as the Factory of the World.

However, all these investment plans were predicated on a clear long-term plan for the future of Hong Kong in its regional road map for development as part of China after 1997. In other words, a stable political future for Hong Kong had to be in place first. The then Prime Minister of the UK, Mrs Margaret Thatcher, visited Beijing in 1982 and met up with China's paramount leader Deng Xiaoping with the specific purpose of discussing the future of Hong Kong. Trade opportunities between the UK and China were also on the agenda, but the future of Hong Kong was the main topic for discussion. It was also apparent that this had to involve the future of Hong Kong Island, Kowloon Peninsula and the New Territories as a whole entity although the ways the trio was ceded to the UK were different. These three parts had become inseparable from one another, and they were all parts of Hong Kong as a single entity. There could only be one jurisdiction. Thus, for the practical reason of governance, June 30, 1997, the expiry date of the 99-year lease of the New Territories, was the only possible time frame on the table for discussions and negotiations, as any resolution of the lease expiry would have to include Hong Kong Island and Kowloon Peninsula.

After intense and extensive talks, an agreement called the Sino-British Joint Declaration was reached and announced in December 1984, five years after Governor MacLehose's first visit to Beijing, and two years after Mrs Thatcher's visit to China.

This declaration stated that the UK would hand over the sovereignty of the whole of Hong Kong back to China, and in return, China would guarantee a high degree of autonomy for Hong Kong and its way of life under the One Country, Two Systems principle for a period of 50 years. Hong Kong would be governed by the Basic Law as defined in the Joint Declaration. This agreement was ceremonially and solemnly signed in Beijing by the UK Prime Minister Mrs Margaret Thatcher and the Chinese Premier Zhao Ziyang on December 19, 1984, with Deng looking on attentively and proudly as a witness. This Joint Declaration was lodged with the United Nations in June 1985.

By any measure, this was a historic moment, not only for Hong Kong but for China as well. The people of Hong Kong would be clear about what 1997 and beyond would hold for them. For China, a piece of land which was ceded to a foreign power in the Century of Humiliation was to be returned to the country in the most peaceful way possible. A historic wrong was properly addressed and put right by China. For the UK, it marked the first time in the history of colonial and imperialist powers that a colony was, instead of being granted independence, as happened to nearly all colonies after WW2, to be ceded back to its rightful parent. Whatever the scepticism and reservation that some in the West might have then, there was widespread acceptance that politically and diplomatically the return of Hong Kong to China was the only way forward.

As a result of this Joint Declaration and the Basic Law, as signed, understood and accepted by the international community, the future of Hong Kong was ascertained. There was a clear path forward in a clearly defined way within a fixed period of time. Hong Kong could start to move again, and move it did, at an incredibly impressive speed! In my view, the economic and civic progress made in this period could be regarded as the Golden Era. According to data from the World Bank, the average economic growth of Hong Kong over this period of 13 years (1984-1997) following the signing of the Joint Declaration was staggering and uninterrupted, registering 6% per annum without any pause. This was a figure few places would have predicted and many could only dream of.

In conclusion, therefore, it is essential to point out that Hong Kong could not have performed so spectacularly well without China. This is why I called this section the China Factor when the imaginative One Country, Two Systems concept was to be put in place in Hong Kong after July 1997.

The Hong Kong Factor

Prior to the completion of the Joint Declaration, the Hong Kong government made a very smart and long-term change in its monetary policy. In October 1983, at the height of the Sino-British negotiations, it was announced that the Hong Kong dollar would be pegged to the US dollar, at a fixed exchange rate within a very narrow range. The aim was to protect the economy and the financial sector from subjecting to the wild swings generated by the currency speculators which were first noted during the Sino-British negotiations, when rumours and misinformation ran high, and the currency speculators smelled blood. As a result of the currency peg, the stability of the Hong Kong dollar was guaranteed based on its pegging to the US dollar and so businesses could make their commercial decisions based on a stable local currency. This policy has since served Hong Kong well.

During the many years of economic growth, the Hong Kong government also prudently started to build up a large and substantial foreign currency reserve, in particular in US dollars, as a defence cushion against currency fluctuations and manipulations by international currency traders and speculators, to protect the Hong Kong dollar, and thus the Hong Kong economy, from these speculators. Some would call these speculators the Wolves of Wall Street. This vast foreign currency reserve acted like a war chest at times of financial attack. In fact, most countries have a war chest, but more often than not, the amount of the war chest is only enough to deal with large swings in currency in an organized and syndicated attack by the speculators. Hong Kong, however, had a substantial war chest. In other words, there was enough ammunition at the government's disposal to protect its financial stability. Every time there was currency uncertainty and speculation on the horizon, the reserve could be used to intervene in the currency market to stabilize the Hong Kong dollar.

It is now commonly agreed by most economists and commentators that the three pillars of economic policies of the Hong Kong government – low direct taxation with no capital gain tax; a small non-interfering, light touch, pro market system of government; and the pegging of the Hong Kong dollar to the US dollar – were the troika that underpinned this Golden Era. These shrewd and sound economic policies have also ensured that Hong Kong does not have any debt and has a vast foreign currency reserve.

This light touch and low taxation did come with a price too. That is, it did not provide the government with an adequate and steady revenue stream. So, a viable and alternative income stream was needed. The government opted to generate the extra revenue necessary for the required infrastructure development needs of Hong Kong by selling land to the property developers through open auctions.

Income so generated by selling land did make a contribution to balancing the budget over the years (in fact, often with budget surpluses) for the government and help to enable it to fund major infrastructure projects such as new subways, new bridges, new rail terminals, and creation of multiple border crossing points between China and Hong Kong to facilitate human movements and logistics transport, which were vital to the economic success of Hong Kong.

The modern international airport at Chek Lap Kok, designed by Norman Foster, had already been planned many years prior to 1997. It was completed in 1997 and fully open in 1998. Every major infrastructure project that the SAR government since undertook was based on the same principle of future proving and safeguarding Hong Kong in maintaining its leading position as Asia's main hub for trading, logistics, information and finance.

The land supply policy of the government was the main reason why property developers were so successful. For years, no other investment was seen by the local people as risk free an investment as in bricks and mortar, which many regarded as a sure win. Since WW2, property development in Hong Kong was the stand-out winner, returns were high while losses were minimal and temporary. There were a few property downturns, but each was followed by an even longer boom. The publicly listed companies which boasted the best returns to the equity market in Hong Kong have always been those which dealt with real estate. There were cynics who pointed out, time and time again, that this heavy reliance on property development might deter Hong Kong from entering into any alternative model for economic development. In fact, they pointed out that this uncontrolled and unstoppable property boom would only lead to higher costs of living, driven mainly by high property prices and rents, and the asset price increase invariably would outpace income growth, imposing a substantial burden on the younger generation. More on this will be discussed in Chapter 9.

There were also significant direct investments made by these property developers in China too, based on the Hong Kong dollar, which is an internationally freely exchangeable currency in the market. These investments went far beyond Shenzhen and spread to every part of China. Many manufacturing plants, shopping malls and high-rise residential buildings in China were invested by Hong Kong developers, fuelling a similar property boom in the mainland. China has such a huge population which, in the last four decades of uninterrupted economic growth, was able to absorb the supplies of private properties. According to the estimation by the Hinrich Foundation published in 2017 (20 years after the handover) and based on Chinese statistics, Hong Kong was the largest source of foreign direct investment (FDI) in mainland China, accounting for a staggering 47% (USD744.8 billion) of total FDI from the period of 1985 (shortly after the Sino-British Agreement was signed) to 2014 (17 years after the handover).

Building on the huge capital needed to fund the property developers and entrepreneurs both in China and Hong Kong, the banking sector in Hong Kong also started to enter into decades of boom. The HSBC and the Standard Chartered Bank, both domiciled in the UK, generated their main profits over the years from China and Asia. Furthermore, as a result of the lucrative business and investment opportunities in China and the expertise so acquired by Hong Kong through its interactions with mainland China, nearly all major US banks and finance houses started to expand into China by setting up offices and even regional headquarters in Hong Kong, all playing their part in making Hong Kong one of the leading international financial centres in the world after New York and London.

These huge investments and financings enabled many Hong Kong companies to play a pioneering role in various aspects of China's developments and facilitate China's trading with the rest of the world. Hong Kong was also able to take a key part in helping mainland China in developing supply chains, designs, marketing and production systems which propelled China to become top in the world in the breadth, depth, know-how, innovation and resilience of its manufacturing sector.

The Human Factor and Work Ethics

There is a common slogan and belief among the Hong Kong people and that is the Hong Kong Spirit. It is very hard to define what this spirit is, but I shall attempt to do so here.

In all these years, I have always thought that Hong Kong, regarded in 1842 by the British as a 'barren rock', had no resources whatsoever. The earlier British saw only one thing, and that was the deep water harbour between Hong Kong Island and Kowloon Peninsula, which they called the Victoria Harbour. They saw this as a perfect conduit, all those years ago, and a great facilitator for sea-based trade, which was the cheapest route for global trade in the post-industrialization era. Apart from that, I failed to see any other resources. After all, the climate could be unbearably hot and humid. The place could always be affected by regular tropical storms from the Pacific Ocean. Flat living or arable land was few and far between. Self-sufficiency in food was difficult and fresh water supply initially was only sustained by the presence of man-made reservoirs, which were never quite enough. Whenever there was a drought, fresh water supply was rationed. I can remember when I was a child, at the time of the most severe drought, we were only given four hours of fresh water supply every four days! Such living conditions could be unbelievably hard. Yet Hong Kong made a success of it. Why? Hong Kong does have one resource – in fact, the only resource – and that is the Hong Kong people.

As mentioned above, the majority of people in Hong Kong were immigrants from China in the early part of the 20th century. At the beginning of 1950, the population of Hong Kong was just over two million. Throughout the ensuing years, the assimilation of the immigrant population into the local indigenous population happened not only seamlessly, but both actually complemented each other, so the sum was greater than its parts. The immigrants from the north, mainly from Shanghai, tended to bring with them a more daring and adventurous spirit to Hong Kong. This is because Shanghai, throughout the 19th century and the first half of the 20th century, was regarded as the most modern and sophisticated city in the whole of China. In fact, one can argue that Shanghai at the time was much more cosmopolitan than Hong Kong as it then was, even though Hong Kong was a British colony.

The indigenous Chinese population in Hong Kong had their roots primarily in southern China, usually from the vast coastal province of Guangdong, where the principal dialect is Cantonese. For someone like me who came from Shanghai, my assimilation into life in Hong Kong is so complete that I can only speak fluent Cantonese and hardly any other Chinese dialects including that of Shanghai, which is basically a very fast, staccato kind of dialect. In general, unlike the northern Chinese, the indigenous southern Chinese in Hong Kong tended to be conservative, hardworking and unassuming, their business practices very much reflecting this ethos. They tended to invest in bricks and mortar rather than making things to sell. This mix of a hardworking trait in the Cantonese and that of the commercial flare of the Shanghainese had provided, in my view, a perfect combination. This combination made perfect sense, it made for the unleashing of the Chinese ingenuity, industriousness, commitment to hard work and self-reliance. It provided a spark to ignite things, and over time, the skills were learned and shared among all and as a result, a sense of civility and shared identity was formed.

During this period, everything seemed to start to come together in a melting pot where all the essential ingredients were there for the formation of an international city. A city which embraced a rich cultural diversity, has progressive prosperity, stability and social harmony. There was a competent government run by able technocrats. These golden years, coming right after the conclusion of the Sino-British talks, prepared Hong Kong well in its international standing and for its return to the motherland in 1997.

What is it, then, that is arguably unique about the people of Hong Kong? I would venture that it is the merging of the Chinese philosophy of hard work, self-sufficiency and looking after one's families, with that of the Western system of liberty and personal freedom to flourish that provided the combination to liberate the unique Hong Kong style of responsible adventurism, for which I mean it is not quite about only being a professional such as a doctor, a teacher or a lawyer, which is the ticket to life in a comfort zone, but it is more about enabling each person to reach his or her own potential, be it an entrepreneur, an artist, a musician, an actor or a writer. Over time, this constellation of talents can provide a rich tapestry of life to enrich the lives of everyone.

It has not been easy. In common with all the other places subjected to colonial rule, it was undeniable that British political and financial interests came first, illustrated by the so-called Big Four discussed in the previous chapter. Nevertheless, since WW2, the concept of an empire and colonization had passed its peak and was on the wane. This provided the opportunity for places like Hong Kong, blessed by the resourcefulness and the ingenuity of its people, all with a modern and outward looking attitude, to flourish.

So, the spirit of Hong Kong can best be described by: against all odds, we can prevail. In other words, a sort of 'can do, fortune favours the brave' spirit.

The Fourth Factor

Now the readers may ponder at this stage what this fourth factor is. Most people in the world may take what I am going to write as a matter of fact and to be taken for granted as a matter of course. Let me explain.

It used to be said that democracy is the best of all 'isms'. This book is not about a debate on the merits and demerits of the various 'isms'. I do not have the knowledge to do so anyway. I do feel strongly, however, that these isms or political ideologies such as socialism, capitalism, communism etc, can best be regarded as a tool for a system of governance. Therefore, how this tool is used depends on, to a very large extent, how it is applied, and as such, it can be misunderstood, misused or worse still, abused. Take Hong Kong as a case in point. In all the years of British colonial rule, Hong Kong did not have democracy, as defined by the West, for which I mean democracy by universal suffrage. It was run as a colony, which practised primarily capitalism, and was politically and administratively always accountable to London.

In 1992, the last governor of Hong Kong, Mr Christopher Patten, five years before the handover, introduced some form of election, via universal suffrage, to elect some members of the Legislative Council in Hong Kong. This was extremely controversial at the time. He, along with London, was accused of conspiring to upset the future stability of Hong Kong by introducing some form of democracy so late in the day, just before the handover period.

What I mean by the fourth factor is, for Hong Kong, there is a governance framework underpinned by the combination of the rule of law, independent judiciary, and freedom of speech. These three pillars do not necessarily mean democracy. Far from it, as many countries thought to be democratic do not have these three functional tools in practice. Yet, these are the key elements of a fair and open society, which Hong Kong was and still is under the One Country, Two Systems model of governance. These elements of the fourth factor, together with the sound economic principle of small government and market approach to trade and commerce, all work together to set the people of Hong Kong free to pursue their own idea of happiness, fulfilment and enrichment.

This governance model offers a well-defined framework for all the people in Hong Kong, in equal measure, a fair and independent judiciary where businesses and consumers have equal rights and access, in a corruption-free society.

Everything is thus accountable, transparent and open. Disputes can be settled and arbitrated in an independent court of law. Information is freely available in this digital age to enable Hong Kong to compete on the global stage. This freedom, especially of movement, speech, and press, is so valued by the people of Hong Kong. These aspects of running Hong Kong were also enshrined into the Basic Law during the Sino-British negotiations, as a means of reassuring the people of Hong Kong that their way of life would continue after 1997.

There used to be a disingenuous and derogatory view expressed by some, who really did not quite understand what makes Hong Kong tick, that Hong Kong people are only interested in making money. This remark in my view is not true or even accurate. It shows a complete lack of understanding or appreciation of the Hong Kong spirit that I alluded to previously.

A more accurate and rational remark would be that, through their self-evident, self-motivated hard work and resourcefulness, the people of Hong Kong created the necessary conditions to provide for themselves a freedom to pursue their own interest and way of life, based on their own ability and the free market principle.

The playing field is level for them all. Prosperity and stability are the main planks of government policy and indeed this is what Beijing repeatedly has alluded to when matters of Hong Kong are discussed. This is what the vast majority of the people of Hong Kong accept and are content with. In other words, the governing and the governed share the same goal.

It is the combination of these conditions that made the Nobel Laureate in Economics Milton Friedman call Hong Kong the only place in the world that testified to how the free market really worked and how it would benefit all those within that system. He pointed out that Hong Kong's per-capita income rose from 28% of Britain's in 1960 to 137% of Britain's in 1996, the year before the handover of Hong Kong back to China. This figure alone represented the achievement of Hong Kong, when in the 1950s and 1960s, it was full of impoverished immigrants from mainland China.

CHAPTER 4

1997 to 2020: Back to China – the Post-Handover Years

This period started from the historical moment when Hong Kong, as a British colony, was officially handed back to China at 00:00 hours on July 1, 1997, in a ceremony attended by official leaders from both China and the UK, attended by the international press. This was then followed by the official inauguration in the morning of the first HKSAR Chief Executive, witnessed by the leaders from China.

For China, the occasion marked the righting of a wrong that was done in 1842. Hong Kong started to face a new era. It was an event which received global attention, as Hong Kong has already established itself as a modern metropolis regarded by many as a city of international fame and achievement. Prince Charles, representing the British monarchy, remarked, during the ceremony, of Hong Kong: "a small coastal settlement ... into one of the greatest trading economies of the world." The mainland Chinese viewed this historic moment with a sense of immeasurable national pride. I myself had the same feeling too, even though I was watching events transmitted live on TV in the UK. The handover was done smoothly and solemnly.

From 1997 onwards, with the blessing of the central government in Beijing allowing a high degree of autonomy both in the administration of Hong Kong and the running of its own economic policy, the people of Hong Kong started to acquire, and then consolidate, all the sophisticated skills required in running a successful international financial centre. Hong Kong was able to progress unabated to excel and compete with the best in the world in the areas of high finance such as investment banking, audit, accountancy, stock market floatation, regulation and supervision. By the 2010s, Hong Kong had joined New York, London, Shanghai, and Tokyo to become one of the top financial centres of the world. The attraction of Hong Kong has been its access to China and its free capital flow, and the stable Hong Kong dollar peg to the US dollar.

Politics and isms such as democracy, communism and ideological doctrines are regarded by most as only a means to an end, but do not necessarily lead to prosperity while proper governance and stability do.

The Asian Financial Crisis

However, this new dawn did not really start without hiccups. There was an immediate challenge, especially since Hong Kong had already made its name as a free capital market where capital can flow freely at the touch of a button in a 24-hour round-the-clock financial interplay involving New York, London and Hong Kong. This would mean that the international speculators were constantly on the lookout to smell blood and make a big bet and a giant killing. Their trade is to make fast money by betting and speculating, playing in the market exactly like the big gamblers in the casino, except that they are even more ruthless than the gamblers, as these speculators are often syndicated, organized, and well informed with the latest economic and financial data. To them, it does not matter who the losers are. It is what capitalism and the market economy are all about, with their upside, which could mean wealth and prosperity, and their downside, which could mean job losses and bankruptcy. The free market, after all, does mean survival of the fittest; greed and ruthlessness are just the unavoidable means employed by some involved in this game.

Thus, the first problem that the Hong Kong Special Administrative Region (HKSAR) faced, in the immediate post-handover period, was a financial crisis towards the end of 1997 which spilt over to a full-blown one in 1998.

This crisis started in Thailand when there was a run by the currency speculators against the Thai baht. Prior to this, Hong Kong enjoyed a continued economic boom, everyone was optimistic and positive about the future because of the assurance offered to the HKSAR under the One Country, Two Systems principle. The local economy was bubbling along nicely but was seen by some as vulnerable and ripe for a correction. In Southeast Asia, there was a syndicated international attempt by short-selling currency speculators to short the markets, and the local currencies in countries like Thailand, Vietnam, Singapore, Indonesia and Malaysia came under attack. This was known as the Asian Financial Crisis of 1997. The IMF (International Monetary Fund) had to step in to help and most of these countries, in trying to fight off the speculators to protect their own economy and currency, had to accept the terms as required by the IMF to restructure their national debt. Some even introduced capital control in fending off such attacks on their currencies.

Then around October 1997, the speculators started to attack the Hong Kong dollar, just when the people of Hong Kong were still in the euphoric state of seeing a smooth and successful return to China. The timing could not have been worse, and if mishandled, there would be plenty of politically motivated opportunists all lining up to make presumptuous and premature negative comments about the whole concept of the One Country, Two Systems, which would destabilize Hong Kong and shake the confidence of the people.

The newly formed SAR government was caught in the first major financial crisis it had had to handle. Hong Kong, in its history, has never had speculative attacks on such a scale. The international speculators adopted a twin-track approach to attack and squeeze Hong Kong. First, they sold short the Hong Kong dollar, believing the pegging of the Hong Kong dollar to the US dollar would be broken. Then they also went into the Hong Kong stock market, especially by short selling the stocks of those public companies whose profits were mainly made in China or the rest of Asia. Overnight the local stock market index, the Hang Seng Index, took an unprecedented plunge, and the listed public companies in Hong Kong saw their stock values plummet. This was a double-prong attack (equities short selling and currency manipulation) with the intention of using the cheap Hong Kong dollar to buy up lucrative assets in Hong Kong when the prices of their shares were pushed down by short selling.

The SAR government, with the support and backing of the central government in Beijing, took brave, decisive and unprecedented action to defend Hong Kong against these speculators. This caught the speculators by surprise. To put it simply, the SAR government dealt with these speculators by playing them at their own game. The SAR government came into the market, became a player, and started to intervene actively by trading against the speculators. Unlike many other Asian countries which needed a bailout by the IMF due to a shortage of foreign currency reserve and national debt, the HKSAR had a rock solid and powerful defence, which was its vast foreign currency reserve with no government debt. So, the SAR government used this foreign currency reserve to bet against the short sellers in the open international capital market to shore up the Hong Kong dollar, while simultaneously counteracting the short selling of shares by directly buying shares in the open stock market. There were two battles, the currency front and the stock market front. Both fronts were fought in the open markets. What was being sold by the speculators was bought clean by the SAR government. These international short sellers met their Waterloo movements. They never once thought that they would come up against a counterparty as strong and as determined as the SAR government. They miscalculated badly by wrongly assuming that the SAR government, because of its long adherence to the economic policy of light-touch and non-interference of the market, would not possibly enter the market itself.

But, therein lies the irony of the speculators' strategy. It was never ever stated anywhere that an open and light-touch society with a free stock market or capital market is exclusively for play by private capital. There was never any rule banning governments from entering the market. Thus, the speculators, in launching their financial attack on Hong Kong, got their fingers badly burnt and sustained massive losses. Some of them even had the audacity to cry foul, accusing the SAR government of abandoning their non-interventionist policy. Their noises were just noises and no one took any notice; not even the most ardent of free marketeers had grounds to complain.

By the end of 1998, the HKSAR had sailed through this crisis. Its reputation of sound and prudent economic policy was enhanced. In an open stock market, buying and selling are allowed by all parties as long as they are done in an accountable and transparent way. The HKSAR won its first decisive battle and was internationally acclaimed.

Things started to improve afterwards, the economy kept growing and by 1999, some two years later, all the stocks that the SAR government owned were sold back in the open market and the government recovered all its investments, with profits. In other words, the taxpayers in Hong Kong won the battle against the speculators. The victory enhanced the financial expertise of the HKSAR in the eyes of the world and the resolution of the SAR government was never to be underestimated or played against by the speculators again. This was the beginning of the realization of Hong Kong coming of age to become one of the financial centres of the world.

Years later, the world had another international financial crisis in 2008, which originated in Wall Street as a liquidity problem by the investment banking industry. I was in the UK at the time. The UK government adopted a similar approach to that of Hong Kong in 1997 by injecting liquidity directly into the UK banks to stabilize the economy and restore public confidence. The only difference between the two crises is that for Hong Kong, the taxpayers were not the losers in the 1997 Asian Financial Crisis and the real economy was not affected. This is in sharp contrast to the global financial crisis in 2008, when everyone was affected, the taxpayers all over the world had lost, public finances were in ruins as a result. Nearly all countries caught in this crisis had to go through a very tough austerity programme to restore public finances over several years.

Throughout this period, when the HKSAR was managed under the One Country, Two Systems principle, there were only three years when its economy experienced negative growth. These were: 1998 following the Asian Financial Crisis as mentioned previously, 2009 following the global financial crisis, and 2020 during the Covid-19 pandemic. The foundations that were laid down for the economic success of Hong Kong since the early 1960s remained unchanged. Hong Kong continued to enjoy economic successes under the SAR government.

Becoming an International Financial Centre

This uninterrupted economic growth enabled massive infrastructure programmes to be achieved. An international airport was commissioned in 1998, new hospitals were built, and new underground networks were added. Furthermore, capitalizing on the manufacturing prowess in nearby Shenzhen, Hong Kong's economy was successfully changed from an export-driven and manufacturing-driven model to a service-led model, with relocation of its manufacturing sector moving inland to Shenzhen and its surrounding areas. In so doing, the economy of Hong Kong can move up the value and skill chain, thus maintaining its status as one of the world's leading trading and international financial centres.

This is no small achievement in a city which really only began its contact with the international trade community in the rest of the world in the latter half of the 20th century. To achieve this status, the SAR government has to guarantee the policy for the free flow of capital in a manner which must be exemplary and even above the international norm. This would mean to have a good banking sector, with proper and open governance, a good audit and accounting sector, a good legal sector, an efficient stock market to raise public capital and an efficient investment banking system to raise private capital, a transparent tax system and above all, a level of professional expertise on par with that of New York and London. Not only that, there must also be a transparent, corruption-free and effective regulatory and supervisory system to ensure fair play and openness, which Hong Kong has. Too much regulation will stifle innovation while too little will encourage wrongdoing. There must be a balance and Hong Kong, by common international consent, seems to have achieved the right balance. Shanghai, another modern city in China, also aspires to be an international financial centre with a maturing stock market, but the free capital flow allowing for the transactions of international and convertible currencies in Shanghai is not as well established and efficient as that of Hong Kong.

Further Challenges

Yet, even though the overall economy enjoyed growth above the global average in all these years, it was not all plain sailing. Hong Kong did have other challenges. There were two public health crises and two political crises affecting its governance.

In 2003, an unexplained and severe respiratory illness appeared in Hong Kong and southern China. This was known as SARS

(Severe Acute Respiratory Syndrome) and the pathogen was identified by the academic staff at the University of Hong Kong as a coronavirus. The crisis lasted for about six months, with 1,755 cases identified (second in the world only to China), and 299 deaths (a shocking mortality of 17%), including some medical staff.

It has to be explained here that SARS was named as a syndrome, which in essence means it is a clinical definition before the causative agent known as the coronavirus was identified. This syndrome was so defined because the patients affected developed rapid onset of severe respiratory problems, often needing medical care in Intensive Care Units (ICU) with the use of ventilators. There was no known epidemiological information at that time on whether mild cases or asymptomatic cases existed. These latter two points are of relevance as they were fundamentally different from 2020 when Hong Kong was hit by the Covid-19 pandemic.

The second health crisis was the aforementioned pandemic in 2020 named by the World Health Organization as Covid-19. This pandemic was also caused by a virus belonging to the same family of coronaviruses, just as SARS. By the end of 2020, there were more than 8,600 infected cases in Hong Kong with 137 deaths reported to be associated with Covid-19. These deaths mainly involved the elderly with comorbid medical conditions. Hong Kong had to go into the lockdown mode. By October, the HKSAR had had to implement three city-wide lockdowns in nine months, with travel restrictions, quarantine for visitors, social distancing, and closure of restaurants and public places. Non-Hong Kong residents were barred from entry into the HKSAR. These measures were very similar to those taken by nearly all the countries in the world. As a result of these lockdowns, for most of 2020, Hong Kong's economy took a nosedive.

It is not known, nor can it be predicted, at the time of writing this book, when the economy will start to recover. The optimists predicted recovery might start by late 2021 while the pessimists predicted the green shoots of recovery would not be seen until 2022. Schools were closed and the public hospital system was overwhelmed. Extra specialist staff were recruited from China to help the SAR government deal with the health crisis, especially in the testing capacity for the virus and the setting up of new isolation facilities.

In 2003, the SARS outbreak in Hong Kong, regarded by most as a regional epidemic, lasted about six months and the Hong Kong economy had a speedy V-shape recovery afterwards before the year end. It is highly unlikely that the same would happen with Covid-19, as it is the first pandemic affecting the whole world. The damage done to the Hong Kong economy by Covid-19 was undoubtedly deeper and quite possibly harder to recover from, with the hospitality, retail, tourist and aviation industries being the hardest hit.

Furthermore, over these years, Hong Kong also went through two political crises of civil unrest. The first one was called the Umbrella Movement in 2014 which lasted for 77 days, and the second one was the anti-extradition movement which started in June 2019. Both these events will be discussed further in Chapter 7.

CHAPTER 5
The Emergence of the Hong Kong Popular Culture

It was Ruskin, the great English art critic, who said: "Great nations write their autobiographies in three manuscripts, the book of their deeds, the book of their words, and the book of their art. Not one of these books can be understood unless we read the other two".

This is a chapter of significant personal relevance, as I am a fan of the Hong Kong culture in nearly all its forms. It may also help to explain how the economic prosperity in Hong Kong since WW2 became an enabler not only for the emergence of a stable, peaceful and civil society but also for the creation of the unique Hong Kong culture. This Hong Kong brand of culture is primarily a very local form of culture which is widely popular with the people of Hong Kong. Various forms of such a culture and its expressions have since won numerous international awards and recognitions.

The Background

Way back in the 1950s and 1960s, there was no local popular culture as such. Hong Kong was a British colony and China was insular from the outside world. I remember that when I was growing up, I was only more familiar with the Western popular culture. For instance, I drank Coca-Cola, listened to Western popular music on the radio, became aware of and enjoyed the rock and roll music of The Beatles and Elvis Presley. Local popular culture did not exist in Hong Kong.

There were certain traditional and regional Chinese cultures still relished by some in Hong Kong. These were operas based on either the northern region of China (Beijing) or the southern region of China (Guangzhou), but they were hardly mainstream entertainment, and certainly not very popular among the young. These operas were very theatrical, the lyrics very hard to understand, and thus did not gain widespread popularity. Chinese art and literature were taught at school but not in depth, nor for that matter, Chinese history. These Chinese operas in Hong Kong were overshadowed by the massive and popular appeal of Western popular culture, which was initially introduced in Hong Kong after WW2 through the radio and cinemas. For the film industry, the blockbusters were without exception Western productions, especially from the big Hollywood studios which produced films featuring western cowboys, adventures with gun fights (the Lone Ranger riding on a white horse came to mind), romantic love stories of the tear-jerking type, or war films about WW2. The actors and actresses, along with some pop singers, became household names in Hong Kong. In other words, in a British colony where more than 90% of the population were ethnic Chinese, Western popular culture took root and was very much the norm.

These social phenomena, however, were not unique to Hong Kong. It was the same in any colonial society, as the intention was to introduce the local population to the Western way of life, in which music and films were the main media. Now, looking back, after all these years, I am beginning to understand why some would suggest this is an illustration of using 'soft power' to influence people. The prevalence and popularization of Western popular culture, in one sense, demonstrates the real meaning of the soft power of colonialism. For me, I freely admit that I was an example of the influence that this soft power had on me as I was more interested in Western rock and roll music and Hollywood blockbusters. I dare say I was not the only one as many of my classmates were the same as me. It is inevitably a by-product of a colonial ruled society where the culture of the rulers came before the culture of the ruled. This soft power covers a wide range of areas from fashion and designs, to music and entertainments, with a heavy influence on the development of the local culture.

In those days, to listen to music, we only had the old fashioned transistor radio. To have a black and white television set was seen as a sign of prosperity and modernity. To have a record player with a speaker, and a personal collection of vinyls, was a real symbol of being cool. Cassette recorders or compact discs did not exist. These days, old fashioned transistor radios, I believe, have become, just like classic watches or cars, collectible items for the bygone ages. When television was first introduced in Hong Kong in 1957, it was a cable service with more than 90% of its programmes made in the West and imported into Hong Kong. Local programmes were few and far between. There was some news broadcast, but that was only for a few minutes. The news was read and there were no newsreels.

As far as I can remember, for the period from the 1950s to the early 1960s, there were only two commercial wireless radio stations and only one cable television channel called Rediffusion Television, a British owned company. The radio stations broadcasted mostly stories told in Cantonese or played traditional Chinese music or Western pop music, as it then was.

Back then, the vast majority of people in Hong Kong, especially the poor immigrants from China, all had to struggle to make a living. Most people then simply did not have the means, the time or the motivation to develop their creative and imaginative skills in writing, broadcasting or music. Hong Kong did not have the talents needed to build its own entertainment industry or popular culture in society. Our parents and siblings were simply too busy making a basic living. Everyone who could work would work, and the young, if bright enough, might be allowed to attend schools and if not, even the very young would have to work too as education was not free. We did not understand then the concept of child labour. The old also worked. The only people who did not work were those who could not work either because of illness or physical disabilities. Times were hard, it was all work and no play.

As already discussed previously, the earlier years of hard times helped the people of Hong Kong to develop a work ethic which propelled Hong Kong forward economically in a way that the world had come to admire. Striving for self-sufficiency and making a living had become the soul of the local people. The Western world, for the first time in history, started to notice that it was indeed true that the people of Hong Kong had a work ethic rarely found in other places. Words like resourcefulness, industriousness and resilience were expressions commonly used to describe the Hong Kong people. These collective attributes were how the solid foundation for the subsequent progress of Hong Kong was laid. Work ethic became the much admired hallmark of the Hong Kong people in the eyes of the world. I was proud to be brought up in such an environment.

Yet, times change and people change too. Human beings always adapt to the change of our environment. It became abundantly clear in Hong Kong that by the late 1960s, there were things in life other than economy and prosperity. Hong Kong must also seek civic enrichment and start to exhibit its hitherto undiscovered creativity and imagination. There was a need to create a Hong Kong brand of popular culture, a culture which would resonate with the life of the people of Hong Kong, just like other cities in China such as Shanghai, Xian or Guangzhou, each having its distinctive local popular culture.

The concept of Borrowed Time, Borrowed Place, though laid deep in the psyche, was beginning to be felt as outdated. This was the start of a sense of affinity and affection for Hong Kong and the beginning of a conviction of an identity that Hong Kong would be our home. We did not feel we were living in a borrowed place. Hong Kong must unshackle itself from this concept. This would be our home and our place of birth for many people as well. We needed to develop our culture as a mark of creating our own identity for Hong Kong. People started to realize that there should be a fertile and flourishing environment for the writers to write, the actors to act, the singers to sing, and the film producers to produce, in a manner that was commercially viable for them to make a living and be successful too. Culture cannot be created overnight. It takes time but nonetheless is needed, without which a society may be seen as hollow and shallow.

Over the ensuing years, as the economy began to boom and the hard work attitude gradually provided the people with a measure of financial stability and security, people started to look for leisure activities to enjoy after a hard day's work.

The 1967 riots and the corruption scandal of the police superintendent Peter Godber case were wake-up calls for the Hong Kong government, which then realised that there was a need to improve the social, recreational, entertaining and cultural environment in Hong Kong. The time had come to develop some form of 'Made in Hong Kong' popular culture as a measure to provide some means of entertainment to the local people in a way that could resonate with them. This could also nourish the talents of those who aspired to be performing artists, sportsmen, writers or broadcasters. The government also needed to be much more open to engage and connect with the public and allow them a chance to express their views. Radio phone-in was encouraged to be a regular broadcasting event and later on regular public forums for civic discussion, which were shown live on TV too.

In 1967, the first free-to-air TV station called Television Broadcasts (TVB) was set up and together with a local big film studio called the Shaw Brothers, started to produce locally made popular films and TV shows. Both proved to be commercially very successful and were very well received by the public. Local news was no longer just reported in the newspapers or on the radio but actually by the TV studios as well. Live broadcasting was introduced and in-depth reporting and commentaries became the norm. As a result, the people of Hong Kong became far better informed and much more active in voicing their own views on local affairs. Their voices were beginning to be heard.

In 1976, a new milestone was established when Radio Television Hong Kong (RTHK) was set up from its predecessor Radio Hong Kong. With a funding model very much similar to the British Broadcasting Corporation (BBC) in the UK, RTHK is a public broadcasting service using various platforms to inform, engage, educate and entertain the people of Hong Kong.

All these institutions, such as RTHK and TVB, turned out to be enormously successful. They were respected as they all grew with the people of Hong Kong. The difference between BBC and RTHK is, BBC charges an annual fee while RTHK, funded by the Hong Kong government, is free!

So, from the late 1960s, Hong Kong as a society saw the beginning of its own popular culture with the presence of a fairly modern media platform comprising newspapers, magazines, television channels, films, and radios, moving Hong Kong up a gear, to what in the present day are called the multimedia world of modern communication, entertainment and information sharing.

As Hong Kong became more prosperous, people also started to travel abroad and in doing so, they were able to broaden their horizons. It was Mark Twain who put it: Travel is fatal to prejudice, bigotry and narrow-mindedness. Many shared their experience by word of mouth, but many also wrote about their travelling experience as a means of stimulating further interest in travelling. Because Hong Kong was a British colony, the people of Hong Kong enjoyed visa- free entry to many places in the world.

The social, economic and civic conditions were thus ripe in Hong Kong, starting from the late 1960s, for it to start its journey of seeking and creating its own form of local culture, which can reflect the way that people live and think. Unlike China, Hong Kong could not claim to have a long history, and the real growing up of Hong Kong only started after WW2, so the culture that Hong Kong could create has to be a popular form of culture based on the ongoing social trend. In the creation of this unique and popular culture, there were several examples which can be used to shed light on its developments.

Newspaper and Publishing Industry

For the newspapers, they started to increase sales not only through mainstream news reporting, but also through adding current affairs commentaries and paying freelance writers to serialize their stories on a daily basis, which lured readers into continuing to buy the newspapers every day for the purpose of following the stories in addition to reading the news. This unique phenomenon of serialization of stories in the newspapers covering not only one serialized story but often multiple stories written by different writers each and every day, deserves some special mention here.

Many of these writers came to Hong Kong from China in the 1950s and 1960s. They had a distinctive style of writing and storytelling by always leaving a twist or a surprise by the end of the daily serialization, so that readers would be hooked and felt compelled to buy the newspaper to chase the story day after day, week after week. Over time, these writers refined their craft to perfection.

These popular stories were often the engine for growth of the newspaper industry. Even though the original aim of such a storytelling method was to boost up the daily sales, their significance went much further than that. This way of storytelling became so popular and so welcomed by the public that it helped to ensure the commercial viability of the newspapers, with extra income brought in by commercial advertisements because of the high daily sales figures. The success of these writers and this very distinctive craftsmanship in writing styles then began to attract the attention of the literary critics in Hong Kong, then China, Taiwan and the Chinese communities throughout the world.

The one writer who stood out with distinction was Mr Louis Cha. He was much better known in the literary world as Jin Yong, which was his pen name. His literary work was based on a firm training in classical Chinese literature and knowledge of Chinese history. He started his writing career after he arrived in Hong Kong in the 1950s, when he initially worked as a screenwriter for one of the local film studios. Over the following decades, he became the standard bearer of this type of popular fiction writing, combining a well-crafted epic against a historical background landscape, often covering periods of turbulence and invasions by non-Chinese from the North or the West in the imperial Chinese history, thus adding a degree of authenticity and nostalgia.

Jin Yong started writing his stories by daily serialization (武俠連載小說) in the newspaper. This was so successful and popular that he not only made a name for himself with a huge personal following, his work also became the benchmark and standard setter. His writings were mainly about those at the margins of society. The plot always combined a mixture of intense human emotions such as love, friendship, loyalty, and touched up a bit by well-known Chinese folklore history and physical fighting of all kinds, but he never glorified violence. The subplot always addressed morality issues such as right and wrong, good and evil, the rich and the poor, the rulers and the ruled, in a way that was both entertaining and addictive. He was, therefore, not only a great story teller without peers, but also a tour de force in creating a new genre that first appeared in Hong Kong. I am, shamefully to admit here, one of those who got hooked. I started to read his serializations in my high school years and once got caught reading in class and had my story book confiscated.

His work quickly spread and became widely popular in the Chinese-speaking world. It used to be said that where there are Chinese, there will be his books (the serializations of the stories he wrote were all later compiled and edited by himself to be published in books, which all became bestsellers among the Chinese-speaking communities). He later became popular also in Japan and Korea where his work was introduced through translation. It was particularly well-received in Japan as some heroes described in his books could resonate with the Japanese culture of the samurais. In the last few years, his work has started to appear in the English-speaking world too, with the most recent one being The Legend of the Condor Heroes. His stories had also been made into films and television dramas, often repeatedly. There was one book in particular which was, as far as I know, made into at least six different versions of TV series in both China and Hong Kong over the decades.

By the turn of the millennium, he was a legend and was indisputably the leader of the pack of those who were regarded as pioneers for the development of the Hong Kong popular culture. To this day, whenever and wherever the writer called Jin Yong is mentioned, the introduction would always say that he was a writer from Hong Kong.

I have personally read and reread his books too. Yet, it is quite hard for me to describe his work to the Western readers. Perhaps one can attempt to explain it as a mixture of Harry Potter and Star Wars, or perhaps a mixture of Lord of the Rings and The Game of Thrones too.

Having so successfully developed himself as a writer of distinctive Chinese fictions, he then became also a very accomplished current affairs commentator of politics in China, Taiwan and Hong Kong. He showed his entrepreneurial flair and capitalized on his fame and popularity by setting up his own publishing company. This had a catalytic effect as the success of his company was arguably one of the main reasons that Hong Kong started to have a thriving publishing industry. This was unprecedented in a British colony where book publishing was insignificant in scale and was based primarily on the English language. For publishing in Chinese, it simply was non-existent in Hong Kong until Jin Yong came along.

Thus he created the first publishing conglomerate in Hong Kong consisting of newspapers and weekly and monthly magazines covering a wide range of topics, not only news and current affairs, but analytic work in Chinese literature, history and culture too, the first of its kind in the world. By modern standards, he would have been regarded as a tycoon. Yet, he was somehow regarded by many Chinese all over the world not as a tycoon but rather a man of high intellect with extensive knowledge and love of Chinese literature and culture.

The peak of his commercial success was when his conglomerate produced a weekly Sunday magazine which turned out to be a must for the people of Hong Kong on Sundays. This magazine was an instant hit when it first came out. For a start, it was apolitical and did not cover news, but did cover a wide range of celebrity gossips, colour photos of lifestyle reporting and trendsetting, reviews on films, music and consumer products, rounded off with light-hearted, well-written articles on the small and trivial matters of life by famous writers and columnists. This was exactly what the people of Hong Kong needed at that time, a magazine published in Chinese, expressed in a sort of nouveau cultural format which perfectly fitted the state of society at the time.

Hong Kong had by then started to introduce a six-day working week. Most people had Sundays off and as common among the Chinese, Sunday dim sum (Chinese delicacies) lunch with family members in a crowded restaurant was regarded as the highlight of the week and a must-do for the week. I was no exception and went out weekly with my mother and siblings, like most others did at the time. To me, it was an extraordinary social observation that, almost without exception and certainly with no exaggeration, each table in the crowded restaurant would have at least one copy of the magazine bought on that very same Sunday. This was the classical display of converting habits into a culture.

For my generation, I can say, with a fair degree of confidence, that my contemporaries, who all grew up in Hong Kong, will remember with fondness the era of Jin Yong. I dare say few would disagree with me here since we would all have at some stage during those years read something either written or published by him.

The Film Industry and Bruce Lee

Then came the blossoming film industry. Going to the cinema to watch a film has always been a very popular form of leisure activity for the people of Hong Kong. During the 1950s and 1960s, all the big box office hits were exclusively Hollywood blockbusters. There were some Hong Kong locally made black and white films, but these were cheap productions aimed at a very small market. These locally made films were fast productions and the quality was poor in general. It used to be said that these films were made in merely seven days! Such local films were never the mainstream, playing mostly second fiddle to Hollywood films and were never screened in the mainstream popular cinemas. However, there were a few successful local colour films that started to hit the box office by the late 1960s, produced by the Shaw Brothers Studio in Hong Kong.

Then it all changed in the early 1970s, with the return to Hong Kong from Seattle of the legendary Bruce Lee. Even though he was born in the USA, he was very much regarded by all as a son of Hong Kong as he had been brought up and educated in Hong Kong until his teens.

Bruce Lee was the one who ignited the global popularity of the Kung Fu (功夫) phenomenon. He started to appear in films made in Hong Kong, initially as an actor but then quickly became an actor/director. His films were full of eye-catching and carefully choreographed bare-handed one-to-one fighting scenes, all designed in such a way as to showcase his very original fast, furious and macho fighting skills. The special term Kung Fu was born, and it was Bruce Lee who was universally credited with bringing it to the attention of the world.

Kung Fu is a special kind of martial arts with speed and power, where offence and defence mingled together at the blink of an eye. In Kung Fu fighting, unlike boxing or wrestling or judo, there is no rule. This practice of martial arts has to be seen to be believed. Bruce Lee was the absolute master and originator. Fighting scenes in most other films were mainly choreographed and edited scenes. But Bruce Lee's fighting scenes pioneered and emphasized speeds and fast reactions with muscular, balanced and graceful movements of the whole body, matched by facial expressions which were full of energy, anger and even hate. This combination of his Kung Fu fighting and facial energy was perfect for modern films in terms of pure visual excitement and entertainment. Thus, he single-handedly introduced these elements in Hong Kong Kung Fu films to the international film industry. He achieved worldwide acclaim and was the one who started a new worldwide genre of Kung Fu films. Such was his legacy that some 20 years later, in the Hollywood blockbuster film called the Matrix, there were some very similar jaw-dropping, amazing fighting scenes. These were all carefully choreographed by a very accomplished Kung Fu instructor from Hong Kong. The main actor, Keanu Reeves, had to be trained as a Kung Fu fighter for this film by this instructor, who should also claim some credit in the worldwide success of this film.

When people, even to this day, talked of Bruce Lee, they associated him with Hong Kong and Kung Fu. Without him, there would not be the world of Kung Fu.

The film industry of Hong Kong then started to blossom into its golden age. Apart from Kung Fu films, Hong Kong also excelled in comedy films (港產喜劇), which were mainly started by the Hui brothers whose stories were mostly about a con man trying to make a living in a tough world. Another comedy actor of major influence was Stephen Chow, who had hits after hits of comedy, and many of his spoken lines were even turned into real life slang, especially among the younger generations. Records of gross cinema receipts kept being broken by these films. The gross box office receipts even put Hollywood blockbusters in second spot during these golden years.

Because of the boom in the film industry in Hong Kong, the craft and expertise involved in film making, such as screenplay, cinematography, directing, acting and storyline moved gradually away beyond the scope of fighting scenes in the Kung Fu films to a more versatile genre of films. Many of the locally made films won awards in various international film festivals.

One genre for which the Hong Kong film industry was particularly famous for was gangster films of the underworld (港產警匪片). In 2002, there was one such film, written, produced and released in Hong Kong, about a police undercover agent in the underworld and a triad undercover in the police force. The film was not only a huge box office hit, breaking all previous records, it also received international acclaim and attention. In fact, it was quickly adapted by a globally well-known director, who shall remain nameless, and who adapted the story into a Hollywood film released in 2006. This film won four Oscars (including one for Best Director and one for Best Motion Picture). The joke was that in his acceptance speech in the Oscar ceremony at the Academy of American Film Industry, this award winning director made a mistake by crediting the original story of this film to a Japanese film instead of a Hong Kong film! Readers would have no difficulty in working out what this film was.

The Television Industry

The television industry also played its part in enriching the local popular culture. Television Broadcasts (TVB), set up in 1967, initially only dabbled in news and sports with some imported dramas dubbed into Cantonese. There was hardly any home-made TV drama. The first drama it produced was a daily show of 15 minutes broadcasted in the afternoon. Yet, the timing of the setting up of TVB could not have been better, as it was right at the tail end of the riots which had so traumatized Hong Kong. The people of Hong Kong were then fatigued with social unrest and this TV station was like a tonic to lift their spirits up by providing them with home entertainment from this free-to-air service. It was a commercial set-up and its revenues were entirely generated by advertising. The TV studio also invested in its production team by establishing its own training school for young actors and actresses, and assembling its own team of modern scriptwriters.

TVB had a landmark programme which was a nightly variety show broadcasted live during the week from 9:30 pm to 11pm. It was called Enjoy Yourself Tonight (歡樂今宵) with studio audience attendance of around 300 people. First aired in November 1967, it was an instant hit which became hugely popular with the public and was seen by some as the must-watch programme every night. Hong Kong had never had a TV show like that. It ran for 27 years until 1994, with a whole generation of people growing up with it or growing old with it. During the 27 years, it was indisputably part of the Hong Kong culture.

In addition, throughout the 1970s and 1980s, TVB also started to produce its own TV drama series with at least 60 episodes for each series. These were also hugely popular. These dramas were shown at prime time and became the dinner companion of nearly every household in Hong Kong. There were hits after hits and these dramas became a way of life for the majority of the Hong Kong people. The productions of these dramas also became a talent pool for the actors, actresses and directors to practise their trade. Many of them became famous idols, and moved from the small TV screen seamlessly to the big screen in the cinema and became household names.

One particular example is an actor called Chow Yun Fat. He was by far the most popular actor and even though he did venture into Hollywood and made some very successful films such as the modern version of The King and I (co-starred with Jodie Foster), he decided after a few years in Hollywood to go back to Hong Kong, where his roots are, and continued to make films based in Hong Kong. He is as popular today as he was then and is considered an icon of Hong Kong.

At the same time while the commercial TV and film industry produced dramas of high entertainment value, the government funded RTHK started also to make its contribution by playing a key part in television production. What RTHK was particularly strong on was the production of documentaries on the history of Hong Kong and current affairs which reported, analysed and commented on various issues of social concerns, often with live audience participation. RTHK also produced, the first of its kind in Hong Kong, a drama series called Below the Lion Rock, with stories which touched upon pressing social issues. The success of Below the Lion Rock was its ability to capture the spirits of Hong Kong in a way no other drama series ever did. It was produced

PATRICK CHU

not like the setting of a typical TV drama but was shot like a film production. This drama series was very well made and its messages on social issues such as the plights of the homeless, the boat people and the forgotten sections of a progressively more prosperous society touched the hearts and souls of many. It spoke for the poor and vulnerable. Because the production team always tried to shoot the dramas on location, it added authenticity to the dramas. The messages to the public were clear, unbiased and never patronizing. The production team stood firm to this principle. The drama told the story as it was and let the audience decide on its merits. It was different to what TVB provided, but it was regarded as one of the best TV shows, winning many awards in international TV festivals. Years later, when I was in the UK, I re-watched some of these episodes, and I was still touched and impressed. For those readers who fancy a trip down memory lane, I would recommend a visit to YouTube.

TVB and RTHK complemented each other well. The former mainly produced commercially successful programmes of high entertainment value while the latter produced programmes with thought-provoking social messages. There was also another commercial TV station called Asia Television (ATV), regarded by some as an attempt to rebrand Rediffusion. It positioned itself somewhere between the successful TVB and the socially conscious RTHK. But regrettably, ATV was closed in 2016 due to commercial non-viability in the modern age of internet and streaming.

The Music Industry

Up to the 1960s, the popular music scene in Hong Kong was dominated by Western pop music. There was some Chinese popular music, but this was Mandarin- based songs with the music and lyrics written and sung by musicians who immigrated from Shanghai to Hong Kong. These migrant musicians were the first generation of musicians that were exposed to and modelled their music on Western popular music, not dissimilar to the American songs sung by the crooners in the 1930s and 1940s, as Shanghai was the first city in China exposed to Western culture due to its very modern, open and metropolitan nature before 1949. These new types of songs were mostly love songs sung exclusively by female singers in Mandarin, and were regarded as, for lack of a better word, more chic and modern as well. This genre of modern Mandarin songs (國語時代曲) first gained its popularity in the 1930s and 1940s in Shanghai and some of the businessmen who immigrated to Hong Kong brought such types of music with them. To people like me, who grew up in the 1960s in Hong Kong, we were probably more familiar with the Western kind of rock and roll popular music exemplified by The Beatles from the UK and Elvis Presley from the USA. In Hong Kong then, the trend in those days was for the pop singers to form their own rock bands, singing rock and roll pop songs in English, with guitarists and drummers.

The first popular song written and sung in the Cantonese dialect (the dialect used by nearly all Chinese in Hong Kong) was actually the theme song of the first mini-TV series produced by

TVB. This started off the genre of Cantonese popular songs, also known as Cantopop (粵語流行曲). These songs were melodic and rhythmic, with well-written lyrics. The catchy and smooth tunes were easy to sing along, striking a real accord with the viewers who often started humming the same tune. As a result of this new trend in locally written and produced music, it offered many well-trained musicians and singers the opportunity to explore new ground. Over the years, these singers, just like their peers in the film industry, became massively popular, with hits after hits. Their records outsold those of the Western popular idols. Some of these singers were also very good concert performers and their concerts were all sold out events. Very soon their fan base and record sales expanded beyond Hong Kong. Not only did they become popular in mainland China but also in many other overseas Chinese communities too.

Special mention ought to be made of a particular singer called Sam Hui, a University of Hong Kong graduate who started his singing career even when he was a student at the university, earning extra money by singing in a dinner bar/restaurant near the campus. He later became a singer/songwriter as well as an actor. Not only did he sing well with his clear, crisp voice, he also wrote lyrics which resonated perfectly with the way the ordinary people of Hong Kong felt. His music could be melodic or rock and roll, but his lyrics were always sharp, witty and often thought-provoking, and for me, some were profound reflections of life too. He seemed to, almost effortlessly, be able to establish a rapport with the people of Hong Kong through his music and lyrics, which no one else could. Some of his lyrics have become immortal lines. Just like Jin Yong in the publishing world, Bruce Lee in the martial arts world, and Chow Yun Fat in the film industry, Sam Hui was their equivalent in the Hong Kong popular music world.

So, from the late 1960s to the early 2010s, there was a real blossoming of the local Hong Kong popular culture embodied in the publishing industry and the entertainment industry including films, television and music. This became a fairly indispensable way of life for the people of Hong Kong. This popular culture of Hong Kong had come of age, with its own form and identity.

Unlike the phenomenon of Beatlemania in the 1960s which I witnessed, there was no mania for this popular culture in Hong Kong as it developed insidiously over a period of time. East meets West resulted in a tapestry with a rich display of artistic and creative talents in various forms. It was endearing and long lasting. This is what made it into an art form.

The main reason, I think, why these popular cultures were so successful was because most people in Hong Kong felt that these cultures represented the way of life in Hong Kong in a way which no other cultures could. They were unique to Hong Kong, so over time, the local people developed a strong bond with these popular cultures. These cultures were all intertwined to become a mark of identity for the people of Hong Kong.

One of the definitions of a popular culture is its ability to transcend boundaries. At their peak, these popular cultures in Hong Kong also spread to and became very popular in China and overseas Chinese communities. So the 'Made in Hong Kong' label was not only about manufactured toys or electronic watches for export, but also the Made in Hong Kong cultures too.

History will see to it that if ever there is an exhibition or museum display of Hong Kong, these popular cultures would be an integral part of the Hong Kong story.

For me personally, to this day, there are songs in which the tunes and lyrics I can still remember clearly and can sing along with easily. There are stories in the books of Jin Yong whose story lines are still very much in my vivid imagination, and there are films in which some scenes and shots are forever imprinted in my mind. I share all these with the readers very happily and fondly, and with great pride. I hope this can strike an accord with the readers in appreciating the importance and the success of these local cultures in representing Hong Kong.

CHAPTER 6
The Success in the Reshaping of its Economy

Before Hong Kong entered into its golden era, its economy was mainly built on an export-led, labour-intensive and low-tech manufacturing sector. In the 1960s and 1970s, Hong Kong manufactured products for export were mainly textiles, watches, toys, electronics, wigs and plastic flowers. The production cost of these was low and so the export price was very competitive compared with that of similar products in stronger and larger economies in the West. This was also the era during which consumer products, retailing and shopping became fashionable and popular. In these earlier periods, Hong Kong did not have a modern labour protection law or minimum wages, thus reducing the overall manufacturing cost of any products. These cheap and well-made Hong Kong products were mostly targeted for export markets in the advanced economies of the West such as the USA, Europe and the UK whose economy was very much at the time driven by the demand for consumer goods.

Climbing Up the Value Chain

As the economy and prosperity of Hong Kong grew over the years, labour costs became higher when more of the working class moved from blue-collar jobs to the less labour-intensive, office-based white-collar jobs. Hong Kong, being a tax-free international port with no tariffs on imported goods, was able to seize the opportunity to promote its advantage as a shopping paradise with goods from all over the world without any tariff or sales tax. Furthermore, the Hong Kong government also started to promote the city of Hong Kong as a tourist attraction. That was the start of the service industry in Hong Kong, what was then also widely termed locally as the smokeless industry.

The views of the Victoria Harbour, the islands, the mountains, the modern high-rise buildings by the waterfront, the tax-free shopping, the position of Hong Kong as an international transport hub in Asia, and the special fusion of the cultures of the East and West, where the mystic and exotic culture of the East was laid bare to the tourists from the West, plus the romantic notion that this was also one of the last British colonies, all combined to propel Hong Kong to reach its height as one of the world's most popular cities for tourism.

Having successfully and unofficially been named by the tourists as a shopping paradise and the Pearl of the Orient, Hong Kong then started in earnest its effort in climbing up the value chain of economic development by transforming its manufacturing-based economy to a service-based economy. Most of the factories in the manufacturing sector were relocated inland to its northern neighbour in China, a city called Shenzhen which was designated by China as a Special Economic Zone (SEZ). The city of Shenzhen, in absorbing the manufacturing transfer from Hong Kong, was thus able to capitalize on this vast investment from Hong Kong, and the support of the central government, to develop from being a small fishing village of barely 60,000 people in the 1960s into a modern metropolitan city with a population of more than 14 million today. And by 2018, its GDP had overtaken Hong Kong.

In the process of transforming the economy model of Hong Kong, one key area for Hong Kong was attaining its position of being one of the leading financial centres of the world, after New York, London and Tokyo. By 2020, information from the Economist published in June of the same year suggested that Hong Kong became the third financial centre after New York and London, and ranked number one in the world in IPOs (initial public offerings) whereby private companies raise capital for further expansion by floating their shares in the stock market.

Hong Kong's success in this economic transformation was mainly due to two reasons.

The first reason is that the core economic policy of the Hong Kong government has remained steadfast over the many decades since the 1950s. The principle is that it should be based on a free market model with light regulation, low income tax (flat rate of 15%), no capital gains tax, no sales tax, and minimal government interference, thus allowing for greater freedom for private businesses and enterprises to make investments based on local light regulations and rules, which in the case of Hong Kong, are stable and transparent. In other words, a very favourable environment for businesses with fewer constraints and red tape is in place.

The second reason is one of timing. Just when the manufacturing industry in Hong Kong started to face difficulties for further expansion such as lack of factory space, labour shortage and rising labour costs, China launched its Reform and Opening Up policy in 1979. And Shenzhen, a designated Special Economic Zone just north of the border to Hong Kong, proved to be a magnet for the Hong Kong manufacturing industry to make further capital investments to expand significantly its scale of production. The manufacturing sector started moving northward, almost en bloc, with few exceptions, and significant cross-border investments were made in Shenzhen and its neighbouring areas by setting up factories with much bigger production capacity. This also enabled Shenzhen to attract a young and willing workforce from other parts of China in search of employment. So, while Shenzhen was able to provide a new infrastructure to meet the needs of a new manufacturing sector, Hong Kong was able to provide for Shenzhen and its nearby regions like Dongguan the investment and the skills in modern factory management, product designs, production and distribution. Over time, Hong Kong gradually became a trading centre for the export of products manufactured in southern China to destinations all over the world. In the 1980s, Hong

Kong boasted to have one of the world's biggest and busiest container port facilities to underpin this substantial growth in handling export products.

At the same time, China also needed to attract significant foreign direct investment to develop its economy under the Reform and Opening Up policy. Thus Hong Kong, having acquired all the necessary know-how of modern finance, became the main centre which could help China to attract the investment it needed, especially in raising capital and foreign currency. It can thus be said that for China to be so spectacularly successful in the modernization of its economy, Hong Kong was in the right place and at the right time to provide the right expertise.

The Profile of the Stock Market

The stock market in Hong Kong and its profiles mirrored this economic metamorphosis and transformation. In the first stage of development of the Hong Kong stock market in the 1960s and 1970s, it was mainly dominated by British owned companies. Then gradually, in the 1980s, as the expertise of the local people grew in the area of high finance, especially in the booming property sector, the listings were noticeable by the presence of Hong Kong-based companies owned by the Hong Kong magnates. And by the 2010s, the blue-chip stocks in Hong Kong were mostly companies based in mainland China whose main operating profits are generated from sunrise industries which deal in areas such as fintech, e-commerce, communications, software applications, biotechnology and pharmaceuticals aligned not only with the production of drugs but also related to the expansion in health-related products. These companies, generating their profits primarily in China, are listed publicly in the Hong Kong Stock Exchange, and some even in the New York Stock Exchange, thus enabling them to tap into the international capital market to fund expansion globally. In 2020, two of the top ten companies in the world as published in the Forbes magazine are companies based in mainland China and both of them are listed in Hong Kong.

Arrival of International Finance Houses

As a result of the successful reforms in China and the financial expertise already developed in Hong Kong over the past few decades, foreign financial houses and investment banks then started to set up offices in Hong Kong. Now nearly all the major banks and investment banks in the USA, the UK, Japan and Europe based their Asia regional offices in Hong Kong, paving their way for doing business with the huge market that China has on offer. Other services have also boomed. These include accountancy and auditing, property developments and realtors, management consultancies, and international law firms. Even private education institutions that teach a United States or British style of curriculum have flourished because of the needs of the expatriates, especially those from the USA, who would wish their children to be taught the American way with a syllabus in line with what is taught in their home country.

These are called international schools as students from these schools can apply directly to be accepted by the US universities. These international schools were set up initially to serve the children of the expatriates who are all senior executives from global companies working in Hong Kong. These schools have also become very popular among the local Chinese students whose parents can afford the high tuition fees.

The success in transforming Hong Kong into an international financial centre did have its challenges and setbacks, notably the Asia Financial Crisis in 1998 and the Global Financial Crisis in 2008. Hong Kong weathered both crises reasonably well, which further enhanced its reputation as a financial centre.

Not only has Hong Kong successfully developed itself into one of the leading international financial centres, it has also maintained its position, certainly in Southeast Asia, as a commerce centre for trading too, even though the indigenous manufacturing sector is no longer a significant contributor to the local economy. According to the data published by the SAR government, Hong Kong, with a population of 7.5 million, ranked as the eighth largest merchandise trading entity in the world exports and imports in 2019, while mainland China, the USA and Germany occupied the top three spots. Over half of its cargo throughput consists of trans-shipments (goods travelling through Hong Kong). Products from mainland China account for about 40% of that traffic. The city's location in the South China Sea has allowed it to establish a transportation and logistics infrastructure which includes the world's seventh busiest container port and the busiest airport for international cargo.

The Role of HKTDC

Even before the economic rise of China after launching its Reform and Opening Up policy, Hong Kong had already started to explore and expand the scope and expertise of its position as an international commerce and trading centre. A good illustration for this would be the Hong Kong Trade Development Council (HKTDC). This is a semi-government organization pivotal to Hong Kong in its role as a trading platform and is arguably the first of its kind in the world. It was set up to showcase to the world the unique efficiency and skills which Hong Kong can offer in trading. The setting up of the HKTDC thus confirmed the foresight of the earlier business community in Hong Kong in the 1960s that trade would be one of the most important economic development tools for Hong Kong.

The HKTDC was established in 1966, the same year that saw the riots which had their origin involving a labour dispute in a plastic flower factory in Hong Kong. The timing of the establishment of this trade development body showed the great visions of its founders. It was a time of uncertainties. Everybody at the time was worried about the riots and the future of Hong Kong, some even chose to leave for good. The HKTDC founders instead opted to turn this crisis into an opportunity as the riots receded after China let it be known that the status of Hong Kong as a British colony be maintained. The core aim of the HKTDC was to connect the business sector in Hong Kong with the rest of the world by promoting the trading expertise and advantages that Hong Kong could offer.

Over the years, the HKTDC's importance and achievements in promoting Hong Kong as a city to do business in are now widely recognized. It has been playing a pivotal role in the economic success of Hong Kong throughout the years, linking up Hong Kong commercially with the rest of the world in a way which the government could not. The HKTDC knew, and continues to know, its way around trade and commerce much better. In other words, it can promote and advertise Hong Kong as a business centre just as effectively as the Hong Kong Tourism Board in promoting Hong Kong as a tourist attraction. The HKTDC now hosts more than 30 trade fairs a year, with nine of them being the biggest of their kind in the world. It co-owns with the Hong Kong government the world-renowned Hong Kong Convention and Exhibition Centre, which was built over reclaimed land and which now stands out as an iconic building by the Victoria Harbour in Hong Kong, much like the Opera House in Sydney Harbour in Australia.

The international scope of the missions undertaken by the HKTDC includes the presence of about 50 offices over six continents. One key area which must be recognized is its role in helping China to implement its Reform and Opening Up policy since 1979. At the time, Hong Kong was a colony ruled by the British, so the Hong Kong government could not have any official status or representation in China even though China was opening up for active trading with the world. However, the HKTDC was able to establish offices throughout China because it was and still is a non-governmental organization. It started to perform important dual functions of promoting China as well as Hong Kong. The international network that the HKTDC has established can help China to link up Chinese businesses with Hong Kong and through Hong Kong with the rest of the world. It also facilitates local Hong Kong businesses to start up and expand their business in China. This is a perfect role of a mediator, for China, for Hong Kong and for the world. Opportunities and know-how are exchanged, learned, and harnessed through the HKTDC. These functions and roles of the HKTDC remain unchanged in both pre- and post- 1997 periods and are arguably even more important today than previously as China's market economy continues to develop and become much more advanced.

Given all the improvements in a city of just over 1,000 square kilometres and with a population of over 7.5 million, how can one quantify its success and calibrate its international standing through other more objective indicators? I think the following may prove to be illustrative:

1. In 2018, Hong Kong was ranked fourth jointly with Germany in the United Nations Human Development Index (HDI), behind Norway, Switzerland and Ireland, while the USA and the UK both ranked in 14th position. The HDI is a statistical composite index of life expectancy, education

consisting of literacy rate and enrolment rate at different levels of education institutions, as well as per capita income. Life expectancy is regarded by many as a direct indicator of healthcare provision and therefore is a measure of the health status in any given society. So this HDI provides additional information about a country to the more commonly used gross domestic product (GDP). The HDI also gives an indication of the twin pillars of a modern society – education and health profile – which the GDP does not.

2. In 2018, 66 million tourists travelled to Hong Kong while in 2011, the number of tourists to Hong Kong was only 36 million.

3. In 2019, the World Economic Forum placed the ranking of Hong Kong for global competitiveness as being the third, trailing only after Singapore and the USA.

4. In 2019, the Heritage Foundation ranked Hong Kong at the top of the world in terms of economic freedom, for 25 years in a row. The Heritage Foundation is a conservative think tank based in Washington with a significant influence on the making of public policy, especially in the USA.

5. According to the Forbes Magazine 2020, Hong Kong has the second highest number of billionaires in any city, just after New York, and the largest concentration of ultra high-net-worth individuals in any city of the world.

6. In 2020, the International Finance Corporation/World Bank ranked Hong Kong as the third in the world for ease of doing business.

CHAPTER 7
The Renowned Public Services

A modern and well-developed city is often judged by the performance, efficiency and accessibility of its public services. This covers a wide range of areas such as public and private transport and its affordability, education service and its accessibility, medical service and its clinical standards, recreational service and its scope, hospitality service, and emergency service. Only when all these services have reached a certain standard can the city be regarded by most as a 'most liveable' city. For Hong Kong, none of the services above fall short by international standards. In fact, Hong Kong has been renowned over the years for these services.

The Public Transport Services

Of all the services mentioned above, the standout star performer among them would be the Hong Kong public transport service. Not only do international visitors marvel at its efficiency, ease of use and low fares, even the local residents give the transport service the thumbs up consistently over the years. If one starts an informal snapshot survey of asking local Hong Kong residents which of the public services they will place in the top spot, it would be a safe bet to assume it would be the transport service. Unlike the education service which is about teaching those who need teaching, and the medical service about healing those who need healing, the public transport service is about the convenience of mobility for everyone every day.

In Hong Kong, because of the high population density, public movement from point A to point B would have caused an all day-long traffic gridlock but for the efficiency of the local subway system known as the Mass Transit Railway (MTR). This mass transit system, covering and providing an extensive network of well-located subway stations, is so efficient that 90% of the people of Hong Kong use it as the main means of transportation. Someone once boasted to me that if one travels between the two stations farthest apart from A to B within the MTR system, it would take no more than 75 minutes. Furthermore, this subway network is well-served with on the road connection by buses, taxis or public light buses which can fetch the passengers after alighting the MTR station to their final destination, if a connection is needed. Such is the way that the buses, MTR and public light buses and taxis are linked and clustered up that the walk to change from one mode of transport to the next takes no more than a few minutes. Also, nearly all the MTR stations are part of a major shopping complex, so shopping for domestic purposes while one is on the way home is extremely convenient.

Whenever I am in Hong Kong and have to attend a meeting or a dinner engagement, I always work out beforehand the public transport route. I can either take the bus or the MTR, whichever is more convenient, and there is always a choice. Personally, where possible, I would prefer the bus as it is comfortable, and I can sit and enjoy the street scenery or do some reading if needed.

There is no need to buy tickets separately for all these forms of transport (unless one takes the taxi) as payment is all done by a prepaid card which works like a smart card. Indeed, I think Hong Kong's public transport system may well have the distinction of being the first in the world to develop and apply such a remarkably impressive payment system. For the Hong Kong people, it is called the Bart Dat Tung (八達通), which in Cantonese means moving seamlessly among places in eight different directions! It is aptly known in English as the Octopus.

Nowadays, the London public transport system also uses a similar system called Oyster, and in fact, it was modelled on the Hong Kong system. The Hong Kong system is even better than that of London as people can use the Octopus card to pay for any shopping they may need from the ubiquitous local 7-Eleven stores, the supermarkets, fast food shops, or any businesses that are linked to the payment system! Cash free transaction is now an accepted norm in Hong Kong, although in this regard, China is even more advanced.

Unlike many other major cities in the world, Hong Kong also offers for the public another popular form of transport and that is the ferries. Hong Kong has many outlying islands and some of them are actually very popular places to live in, so there has to be a very efficient ferry system connecting these islands with Hong Kong and Kowloon. In particular, the ferry ride across the Victoria Harbour is truly a wonder to behold. The most famous and iconic ferry service between Kowloon and Hong Kong Island is known as the Star Ferry - the ride is truly an experience not to be missed or forgotten. One can see the beautiful skylines from both the Hong Kong and Kowloon side. Whenever I am in Hong Kong, I never miss the chance of taking the ferry if the occasion allows; it gives me a chance of catching some fresh air with a sea salt smell, which is refreshing, while being blown over by the harbour scene. For me, it is also a personal journey down memory lane as from the mid- 1960s to early 1970s I took this ferry daily to attend school for seven years.

Another distinctive hallmark of the public transport system in Hong Kong is the combination of the MTR, buses, ferries, public light buses and taxis, which, though owned and run by different companies, are not designed to compete with one another but rather, complement one another to achieve maximum efficiency with short travelling time, all at very reasonable fares.

Furthermore, in many countries in the West, public transport services tend to be reduced or even stopped at festive times, such as Christmas in the UK. But in Hong Kong, it is the other way round. Public transport service hours are extended for key occasions such as Christmas, New Year's Eve and Lunar New Year for the convenience of people going out to parties, or to watch fireworks in the evening, or visiting families and friends. One other service which must be mentioned is the assistance offered to the disabled. If there is a passenger in a wheelchair, the MTR will provide a special attendant to help this passenger board and alight the subway trains, and for the bus service, the driver will come off the bus to lower a ramp at the door for the wheelchair user to get on and get off the bus. I have not personally witnessed this o n the London Underground.

It is also a sign of a well-run public transport service system that whenever there is a tropical storm approaching Hong Kong, all public transport services, based on the advice and forecast by the Hong Kong Observatory, would inform the public at least a few hours before their services are suspended. This will give people plenty of time to go home safely, not in a rush, but calmly and orderly. The MTR also maintains partial operation even during typhoons. It never fails to impress me every time this has happened in the past nine years of my working life commuting between Hong Kong and China.

During all these years of commuting between and living in Hong Kong and Shenzhen, I had friends who always advised me that I should get a car, to which my standard reply would be: I don't need to own or drive a car in Hong Kong, with all the stresses associated with traffic congestion, looking for directions, parking, maintenance and insurance. One's quality of life, in my view, is actually enhanced by not owning a car. I once calculated, as a self-reassuring exercise, that the yearly running cost of owning and driving a car in Hong Kong is about six times that of owning and driving the same car in the UK. In the UK, driving is often necessary, but in Hong Kong, driving is possibly a relative luxury.

The Education Services

The education system in Hong Kong is also of high quality. Both public and private schools are highly regarded by international standards, though the latter is much more expensive. Most schools are free and government subsidized. Some exceptionally high standard schools opted to run as privately funded entities, which means their admission policy is independent and not subject to government quota. These schools offer the same curriculum as government schools, but admission to these schools is highly competitive. Often the parental preparation in getting their children into these schools starts well before the kindergarten stage! And acceptance into the top primary school or kindergarten will require tests and interviews for the kids. The idea here is to pick the best and brightest at an early age, a practice which does come in for some heavy criticism.

Then there is another type of school called international schools which offer a smaller class size and a curriculum more in line with the Anglo-American model, with strong emphasis on extra-curricular activities such as sport, arts and music. These international schools have become a distinctive hallmark in Hong Kong. They were originally designed to cater for the needs of the children of expatriates from the UK, USA and Europe, and graduates from these international schools have a better chance of getting tertiary education in the UK, USA or Europe as their scholastic achievements or scores are recognized abroad.

In recent decades, these schools have become very popular even with local Chinese parents who hope their children can have an easier option to go abroad for their tertiary education. The one drawback, if such a word can ever be used in private education, is that these international schools are very expensive. It has been estimated by Edarabia that the cost of such private education in Hong Kong can amount to HKD3 million per child and averaging about HKD180,000 per year, and these figures do not even include university tuition or boarding fees. Most of the teachers in these international schools come from overseas and are highly qualified. As these schools are profit-making organizations, having students with well-off parents can ensure their commercial viability. Many of them have additional fundraising activities, which are widely supported by the parents, and some even require a pre-school deposit, like a bond, to book a place even before the child enters into school age. Hong Kong has about 537 local schools and 44 international schools, so the overall competition to get into these international schools can be quite fierce.

There is therefore a wide variety of choices in both the public and the private sector for education, depending on the ability of the children and the financial means of the parents. The access of every child to education is guaranteed by the SAR government. This combination is a highly successful one, with the principle that no child is left out or left behind. But it is also a very competitive one, which, bizarrely perhaps, is more in the mind of the competitive and protective parents rather than the child.

Hong Kong also enjoys high quality tertiary education. There are altogether 20 degree-awarding higher education institutions of which eight are government funded. For a city with a population of 7.5 million, it boasts three of the top universities in the world according to the Times Higher Education, with the University of Hong Kong and the Hong Kong University of Science and Technology within the top 50, while the Chinese University of Hong Kong ranked just outside at 53. This is manifestly a remarkable achievement and no city in the world with the same population has achieved that. Universities in Hong Kong use English as the medium of teaching in most of their courses. All the courses on offer are well-known and respected outside Hong Kong. In recent years, many Chinese students from the mainland and overseas students from other countries have opted to come to Hong Kong for their tertiary education. The university tuition fee here is very low since the institutions are government-funded.

The Medical Services

The third main public service in Hong Kong which needs to be discussed is the medical service. The system here primarily is not dissimilar to the National Health Service (NHS) in the

UK, since Hong Kong was a British colony until 1997 and hence its medical service was mainly modelled on the British system. This in essence means that every Hong Kong resident is entitled to receive free medical care, funded and underwritten by the government, which pays for it through general taxation. The SAR government, unlike its UK counterpart, does not levy any national insurance tax to provide extra funding for state benefits, though it has started to encourage the public to take up the new government-backed voluntary health insurance scheme which was introduced in the last few years. The main difference between the Hong Kong and the UK systems is that Hong Kong also has a thriving medical service in the private sector with well-run medium-sized private hospitals. Just like the education sector, the standard of both public and private medical services is high, on par with any healthcare systems in advanced economies of the world.

The main problem faced by the public health sector is not the standard of care, but rather that the provision of healthcare cannot keep pace with rising demands, especially in an ageing society like Hong Kong. Often patients with non-life-threatening conditions such as cataracts or arthritis requiring surgeries have to wait for months, may be years even, before they can be tended to in the public sector. For expensive treatments such as new anti-cancer drugs, there is an additional co-payment system which means patients have to self-finance the extra cost.

Nearly all the medical and nursing staff are trained in Hong Kong. Professional staff from overseas have to undergo a licence examination in order to get a licence to practise.

For medical training, there are two medical schools, one at the University of Hong Kong and the other at the Chinese University of Hong Kong, and together the two universities produce a combined total of 400 medical graduates a year. By modern standards, it is way short of what a society with an ageing population like Hong Kong needs. The reputation of medical education in Hong Kong, which is taught in English, is universally regarded as one of the highest in the world. To support this, the tertiary education institutions also provide degree courses for professions allied to healthcare, such as nurses, pharmacists, physiotherapists, radiographers, and laboratory technicians. The standards of these professions are also high.

This dual system of medical and educational services with both private and public sector provision enjoys a high degree of public acceptance, as the private sector can offer an option to those who can afford to pay, thus freeing capacity to those who cannot afford or may not be willing to pay. Both systems are competently run and enjoy a high degree of confidence with the public.

Thus, the necessary and essential pillars of a modern society, such as a thriving economy with increasing prosperity of its people, a comprehensive education system to equip its people with knowledge, and a high standard healthcare system to ensure the health of its people, backed by an uncorrupted and efficient civil service to serve all the people, add up as the collective reasons why Hong Kong scores high in the Human Development Index rankings.

CHAPTER 8
The Philanthropists and the Community Benefactors

Notwithstanding its wealth, Hong Kong, just like many other modern cities, has its fair share of poor and vulnerable people. The financial burden of helping these people cannot be expected to be shouldered completely by the Hong Kong government especially since Hong Kong did not have, or could not afford to have, a very advanced social safety net policy to protect those who are unemployed or unable to work. This lack of a European-style social welfare system, which in Europe is funded primarily through a higher rate of income tax, has always been a hallmark of Hong Kong which has distinguished itself since the early 1950s for its relatively low and stable income tax policy.

This free market laissez-faire, low taxation approach has been practised in Hong Kong with great success. The main argument from those economists and politicians against a social safety net provision, or social entitlement as it is called in the USA, is that such provision, through the means of a higher taxation base on income to fund social welfare, may serve as a disincentive for the individual to make maximal personal effort, leading to a very negative mindset of 'the more I make, the more tax I have to pay'. It may even, perversely, lead to a welfare dependency culture. Economy (GDP) grows best when a free, open and competitive market is provided in an environment where individuals have the freedom to pursue prosperity. The free marketeers were pioneered by a group of economists of which the most famous was the Nobel laureate in economics Milton Friedman from the Chicago School of Economics. Furthermore, this school also favoured free trade, small government and monetarism. It also proposed that large government, and hence over-regulations, may often perversely get in the way of economic growth.

This was in sharp contrast to the other post-WW2 model, which was the popular social democracy model, mainly in Western Europe and the Nordic countries, in which government would shoulder the obligations to the poor by providing a more generous welfare system through higher taxation. Such safety net and social welfare policies, as practised in the Nordic and Western European countries, were at one stage the envy of the world. Not being a professional economist, it is hard for me to comment with great scholarly insight and vigour on the merits of these two systems. It seems to me the free market, small government model can create economic growth while the safety net model may create perhaps a fairer society.

In the absence of a social safety net in Hong Kong, those who could not get a job would be trapped. Their life often had to depend on handouts from families or friends. Some might even resort to crime. In Hong Kong during the 1950s and 1960s, it was not uncommon to see beggars begging for food in the streets, or even open street robberies. It was only in the 1970s that some forms of social welfare policies were gradually introduced.

Thankfully, because of growing prosperity in Hong Kong over many decades, there was the recognition that the needs of the poor must be addressed. With the increasing prosperity in society, there came a gradual emergence of a feeling of social obligation to the less fortunate. The rich and the comfortably-off started to carry out, and continuously to do so in these days, numerous acts of charity. This was, and still is, a distinctive feature of life in Hong Kong. As a result, many schools, hospital buildings, community centres, and research buildings in universities in Hong Kong were donated by and named after the benefactors. There are also many voluntary groups forming charitable foundations to help targeted underprivileged groups in society. Among these, four of them stand out, and I call them the community benefactors because of their long history of serving for the benefit of the public in Hong Kong. These are the Tung Wah Group of Hospitals (東華三院), the Po Leung Kuk (保良局), the Community Chest of Hong Kong (香港公益金), and the Hong Kong Jockey Club (香港賽馬會).

Tung Wah Group of Hospitals

The Tung Wah Group of Hospitals, with a history dating back to 1870, is the oldest and largest charitable organization in Hong Kong. It provides extensive education and community services through its 194 service centres spread across Hong Kong.

The Tung Wah Group of Hospitals has its roots as an organization that was brought into being by a group of successful and enthusiastic local Chinese businessmen in Hong Kong in its early colonial period. Among the group, Tung Wah Hospital located on Hong Kong Island is in fact the first hospital established for the Chinese public in colonial Hong Kong.

The historical reason for the formation of the Tung Wah Group of Hospitals was the arrival of the bubonic plague from China. Many local Chinese were affected due to poor sanitation and tragically, most of those who died were so poor that their bodies were not buried but simply abandoned in the streets. So the local well-off Chinese got together to form this organization, initially to help bury the dead, then later extended it to provide healthcare service as well. To this day, the Tung Wah Group is still very much active in the community by being an integral part of Hong Kong's educational and hospital services. Presently, the scale of its operation is unimaginably larger than the past. It has become such a key plank of the local education and medical services that a significant part of its funding is now being provided for by the SAR government.

Po Leung Kuk

The Po Leung Kuk was originally founded as the Society for the Protection of Women and Children in the 19th century when abduction and trafficking of women and children were widespread in Hong Kong, indeed in China too, to provide for the rich life-long female servants called Mui Tsai (妹仔), a sort of female slave bought at a very young age, often pre-adolescent and uneducated, to serve the masters who bought them. These Mui Tsais (meaning young maids), sadly, were all illiterate as no one provided them with an education. The Po Leung Kuk was set up in 1882 to deal with this terrible and most uncivilized of the Chinese way of life. The Kuk, which in the Chinese language means a kind of bureau, was there to look after these poor, abandoned girls, who often arrived as young orphans. The Kuk protected them from being snapped up as Mui Tsais. It provided a safe sanctuary for them where they could have shelter and education. This practice of course has now long ceased to exist, but the Po Leung Kuk has continued to function as a charitable organization in promoting various benevolent social projects. It now has over 300 units providing a wide range of services including social and educational, as well as acting as recycling centres, recreational and cultural centres, with annual funding chiefly from the SAR government.

Community Chest

The Community Chest of Hong Kong is another independent, non-government-funded, non-profit organization established on 8 November 1968 in Hong Kong as an aftermath of the massive destruction and havoc wreaked by a typhoon. As one of the most important charities in Hong Kong, the Community Chest serves as an umbrella organization providing grants to a wide range of community projects and agencies; 100% of its funds are used to enhance local social welfare services without any deductions for administrative costs, which are funded by the Jockey Club. It runs fundraising charity events such as Walk for Millions, corporate-sponsored half marathon, TV variety shows, and flag-selling days. In 2019/2020, it allocated over HKD180 million to its member agencies.

Jockey Club

The biggest of all the community benefactors is the Hong Kong Jockey Club (HKJC). The club is one of the oldest institutions in Hong Kong, founded in 1884. In 1959, it was granted a Royal Charter and renamed The Royal Hong Kong Jockey Club (英皇御准香港賽馬會). The institution reverted to its original name in 1996 due to the transfer of sovereignty of Hong Kong to China in 1997.

It is to this day an exclusive private members-only club. Admission to be a member of the club is through initial nomination by other members and then election by voting members. Not all members have voting rights, which are available only to those with good and senior standing in the club. Although horse racing is its main activity, the Hong Kong Jockey Club also provides various food and beverage, social, sports and recreation facilities to its approximately 23,000 members.

It is generally hard to become club members, and it is more or less restricted to people with good standing in society. Therefore, it is regarded by the Hong Kong people as a marker of attainment of social status. Ironically, a passion for horse racing is not a criterion for admission to be members. People from a privileged background, professional classes or well-connected businessmen generally stand a much better chance of successful application to become members.

Only its members can enjoy the various services that the club offers. Even its membership types can vary from ordinary non-voting members to voting members, with the highest class being the directors of the club. The latter group usually consists of the richest people or those with the highest social standings, or those who are influential in their own fields and in the community. To be a director of the Jockey Club was seen by many as the true elites of colonial Hong Kong and even in the present day HKSAR.

But social status and elitism aside, one should not underestimate the scale and the importance of the charitable work that the

Jockey Club has done for Hong Kong over the years. Its regular and huge contribution to charity in Hong Kong is quite unique and no other gambling institution anywhere in the world can be compared with it. The club is independently run by salaried professionals appointed by its board. Its social standing in Hong Kong serves as a model on how a private club can play such a key benevolent role for the lives of the people in the city where it operates. The Jockey Club operates only in Hong Kong and does not have any overseas affiliations. It is well respected by the people in Hong Kong throughout all these years.

First and foremost, even though it runs horse racing and is licensed as the only betting institution in Hong Kong, it is, by its own charter, a non-profit organization. This is the club's key difference from other forms of betting institutions, such as those in the neighbouring city of Macau, which is now regarded as the Las Vegas of the East with its glitzy and modern casino hotels.

The Jockey Club in Hong Kong holds a government-granted monopoly in providing betting on horse racing, the Mark Six lottery, and fixed odds betting on overseas football events. The organization is the largest taxpayer as well as the largest community benefactor in Hong Kong. The Hong Kong Jockey Club Charities Trust made a record tax contribution of HKD23.3 billion to the SAR government and approved donations of HKD4.3 billion in the financial year 2018/19, to support and help fund the different needs of society and contribute to the betterment of Hong Kong. The club also proactively identifies funds to develop projects which anticipate and address social issues and pressing needs in Hong Kong, such as the setting up of health clinics, residential homes for the elderly, hospice care homes, and sporting amenities.

Apart from these big four community benefactors in Hong Kong, there are many other individual philanthropists who have made significant private and personal donations to schools, hospitals and universities. Many of these philanthropists also made extra donations in times of need such as during the recent Covid-19 pandemic in Hong Kong, when cash donations were made to provide healthcare equipment, personal protective gear and free masks for the local people. As mentioned in Chapter 2, there are families of philanthropists who have consistently made huge donations to various charities. These families became household names and their benevolence towards Hong Kong is much appreciated by the public, and these are the Kadoorie family, the Ho Tung family, the Li family, the Kwok family, the Fung family and the Tang family. For these families, both their business acumen and charitable work have become household folklore. Of equal significance is that there are numerous other families who have over the years donated possibly as much, but many of whom have chosen to remain anonymous. Charitable donation and voluntary work are very much part of life in Hong Kong, a point which is perhaps scarcely mentioned or appreciated in the Western press.

At the end of 2019, there were around 15,700 charities registered by the Inland Revenue Department in Hong Kong. It used to be said charity begins at home and for a small place like

Hong Kong, the charitable spirit of the Hong Kong people has much to be admired. In the aftermath of the devastating earthquake in Wenchuan County, Sichuan Province in China in 2008, the people of Hong Kong made a staggering HKD850 million donation to help the victims of the earthquake. Of this amount, the largest single donation from Hong Kong came from the Hongkong and Shanghai Banking Corporation (HSBC), amounting to HK$220 million, reflecting why most local people regard the HSBC as their own bank. Today some would simply call it the Hong Kong Bank even though it is domiciled in London. For the record, this was the world's largest non-governmental donation ever made on a per capita basis to this tragic event in China.

CHAPTER 9
The Challenges

All societies face challenges. Life is never as smooth as one would hope for, and societies are no exception. Hong Kong does have huge challenges despite its phenomenal successes so far. Some would even argue that these challenges are almost unsurmountable.

The question and debate that may need to be had is this: What are the real challenges facing Hong Kong? Does the adherence to the free market economic dogma which has served Hong Kong so well for so many years have any long-term side effects which may work against the interests of Hong Kong in a fast changing world? Would the prosperity which Hong Kong so enjoys, paradoxically, place Hong Kong in a comfort zone that would foster a sense of complacency that all would be well as long as the free market economic principle is adhered to? If so, does the prosperity that Hong Kong enjoys bear any causal relationship to the challenges that it faces?

This chapter mainly focuses on these challenges with an attempt to explain in some detail how they came about and hopefully may shed some light on the possible ways such challenges can be managed.

Housing

Topping the list of challenges for the great majority of the younger generation would be housing. Property prices and rental costs in Hong Kong are among the highest in the world. Decades of economic growth in Hong Kong has led to a long and continued housing boom. Therefore, a vast significant proportion of personal wealth and assets has been acquired through property buying and selling. Investment in bricks and mortar in Hong Kong has always been regarded by many as the safest investment with the highest returns, especially when no capital gains tax or inheritance tax is levied. It has always been seen by many locals as a one- way bet in making money. Consequently, one of the key markers for wealth and tools for generating wealth in Hong Kong has been the buying and selling of properties, based on the investment psyche of the local people. This observation is in sharp contrast to the rest of the world where wealth is created by much more diversified means.

Over time, the property developers have become tycoons. Without any exception, the tycoons in Hong Kong cannot be truly regarded as modern entrepreneurs because their business was only real estate business, without any true innovations or creative skills. Rather, they are extremely smart and daring property developers, using the same business model over decades since the 1950s. To their credit, these property developers shrewdly saw a growing market for housing based on the growing prosperity of an increasing population. They astutely identified that the building and provision of private housing would have huge potential profitability and thus made huge investments in it. They consistently invested in bricks and mortar and re-invested the profits to build more. They accumulated their fortunes by bidding for land to build shopping malls, housing estates and commercial properties. The sites they acquired were all served with the first-class public transport system or had the potential to be well served with public transport. By doing so, they helped to relocate the newly emerging middle class to purpose-built residential areas. This led to a boom in property prices which in turn enticed many private investors to become buy-to-let owners, attracted by the ever- increasing rentals. This buy-to-let investment strategy in properties remained successful consistently over the years. Over the last few decades, property prices kept going up, with only very brief and reversible short-term corrections along the way. In addition, this buy-to-let way of making money is relatively easy to implement. This investment strategy generates regular income which is free from any capital gains tax when the property is resold.

By 2020, Hong Kong properties had become the most expensive in the world, according to Statista, with an average property price of USD1.25 million. This average price has to be taken with a note of caution as it is only the average of all the properties for sale and does not take into account the average size or the location of the property. In other words, the average figure here may not indicate the huge price range between an upmarket and a downmarket area. The buy-to-let phenomenon, which was once popular in Hong Kong, now yields a return of barely 2.35%, reflecting that even this trend has begun to recede as the capital outlay required for buying a property is too high and the low rental yield has started to take the shine off, seen as measly by those who once favoured the traditionally popular buy-to-let approach.

Because of the high housing costs, many young people and perhaps even the middle class cannot afford to buy any properties, unless they receive financial assistance from their parents. According to the Census and Statistics Department in the HKSAR, owner-occupied housing units in 2020 made up 58.6 % of total housing units while renter-occupied units made up 30.4%. The rate of ownership was 91% in Singapore, a city which is often used to compare with Hong Kong. The owner-occupier rates in China, the USA and the UK are all higher than Hong Kong, reflecting the fact that even though Hong Kong may have a higher per capita income, its property prices are beyond the reach of many people.

As a result, those who own properties in Hong Kong would see their assets keep going up in value (assets inflation) while those without properties are trapped with no assets. The more the price goes up, the more these assets are worth, leaving those without such assets further behind and difficult to catch up. Over time, this has led to the building up of significant income inequality which is becoming harder and harder to overcome.

Income Inequality

Let us turn our attention to the Gini coefficient, which is an index used commonly as a crude measure of the difference between the rich and the poor in a society, with zero indicating equality and 1 indicating inequality. In 2018, the Gini coefficient in Hong Kong was measured as 0.539. This index was the highest in 45 years since records began. And for comparison, in the same year, the US had a coefficient of 0.411; Singapore, which is Hong Kong's main competitor, had a coefficient of 0.4579; while the UK had a coefficient of 0.328. The income inequality in Hong Kong, together with its ever- escalating property prices, does mean that ordinary working people in the middle-income class can hardly afford to buy a decent flat. The significance of the relatively high Gini coefficient is even more magnified when one considers another statistic. The IMF (International Monetary Fund), in its ranking of Gross Domestic Product (GDP) per capita adjusted for Purchasing Parity Power (PPP), placed Hong Kong as the tenth highest in the world in 2020. This is a unique phenomenon in Hong Kong: a high Gini coefficient with a high GDP per capita does tell the story of a structural problem in the HKSAR which is its income inequality.

In most other advanced economies, a couple earning an average income normally would have a decent chance of owning a property which, by the usual standard in the UK, means a three-bedroom semi-detached house with a small garden. In Hong Kong, surveys after surveys reveal that the main financial burden or outlay of any working person is either rent or mortgage payment. According to the estimate by one brokerage house in Hong Kong, the mortgage payment in 2018 averaged 60% of gross income and was likely to go up to 70%. In the UK, the average was about 20%.

For those working as manual labour or those with low incomes, their chance of having a safe and clean living environment is even harder, almost impossible even. For those at the lowest of the social ladder, their living conditions can even be regarded as squalor-like. The government does try to build more public housing, but the demand far exceeds supply. In addition, supply of land is in the hands of the SAR government which auctions the land, while the supply of new residential properties is in the control of the property developers who together act like a cartel in controlling the market. Often, these property tycoons would buy up the auctioned land, but then they would proceed to hoard up the land that has the potential for residential development; this is an attempt to control the market, so the property prices can be kept high.

Most young people either live at home with their parents or rent a tiny place. If any of the younger generation does happen to live in an owner-occupier flat, it is far more likely that this has been acquired through significant financial help from their parents. This social trend has acquired a new name called 'the parental bank'. In an essay published by the Economist in 2020, it was estimated that up to 40% of the debt of the younger generation today may be financed by their parents. There is no known figure for this for Hong Kong, but one can reasonably assume that it is much higher! This parental bank, compounded by the fact that Hong Kong does not levy inheritance tax, makes it more natural that the net wealth of a family is passed down the generations. In other words, wealth is kept within the family both before and after death. So, it is more than likely that if a working person on an average income does own a property, it is not through the generosity of the banks which provide the mortgage but rather it is financed and pump-primed by their parents.

Therefore, this income inequality in Hong Kong is regarded by many economists and social scientists as structural in nature, because the rise in income cannot be expected to catch up with the rise in cost of living, especially when it comes to the issue of housing. It is also structural because of the post-WW2 economic policy of the colonial Hong Kong government in adopting a pro-business, low tax, laissez-faire approach, relying on the free market principle to sustain economic growth and not taxation to address social issues.

By and large, this economic policy has served Hong Kong very well and indeed, since the start of the 1970s, there have been progressive improvements in social welfare provision.

Unfortunately, among all its successes and improvements, the government failed to implement a well-planned and comprehensive long-term housing policy. Short-term financial gains in property developments by the tycoons got in the way and at the expense of a sustainable long-term housing policy.

This is the main reason for the unique problem in housing, as the urgency of resolving public housing shortage was never quite a policy priority of the government. Over the years, rightly or wrongly, the government was seen by many as being too focused on safeguarding a profit-driven business environment while the supply of land for housing developments was too tightly controlled. Indeed, some would say this restriction was intentional and was in cohort with the major property tycoons to make sure the supply and demand market principle was always tilted in favour of the supply side.

The tight control of land supply, together with years of the grossly inadequate provision of public housing (the waiting time for the allocation of a public housing unit is about five years) would clearly work in the interests of the property developers instead of the public. The net effect is that the majority of the public can only look to the private market for their housing needs, and as time goes by, the price of property would have increased to a level which is beyond the means of most people, as the growth in wage income cannot catch up unless there is parental help.

The Gini Index does not lie. I have never seen or heard anyone in Hong Kong denying the existence of income inequality. To prove this, one only needs to visit the slum areas in Hong Kong and see how those less fortunate live. It is quite heart-wrenching and shameful even. Yet these people are not necessarily jobless, they do have a job, though often low paid and manual in nature. And for those with no jobs and living on the barest of social welfare support, they are most likely to be living in more squalor-like conditions.

Worthy of special mention is what is known as subdivided units (劏房) in Hong Kong for the low-income earners. These subdivided units (also called subdivided flats) are a unique and ubiquitous type of rental housing found in Hong Kong. They are small flats which are further subdivided into two or more separate units to house more people. The flats' original partition walls are usually removed and new partitions are erected, with very basic cooking (a single stove) and sanitary provisions, internal drains added or altered. These partitions and modifications often compromise the building's safety and hygiene, and at times of outbreak of infectious diseases, these places become a paradise for viruses and bacteria. Such units in Hong Kong can best be described in English as: dissecting an already small flat into even smaller units by erecting partitions. In other words, using partitions as the dissecting knife, and it offers the minimum of privacy at the expense of safety and hygiene.

It is estimated that about 280,000 people live in these subdivided flats or other similarly undesirable conditions, mostly located in old residential buildings. Many subdivided flats are even smaller than prison cells in Hong Kong. According to a study by the Society for Community Organization, people living in subdivided flats are mainly unemployed citizens, low-income families and new immigrants. The median living area per person of a subdivided flat was found to be 3.7 square metres for a small suite and 2.8 square metres for a cubicle in 2009.

More shameful is the cage home, which essentially means a bunk bed enclosed with a metal cage. Even though this is a left-over from the earlier decades, the 1950s and 1960s, when Hong Kong was bulging with massive immigration, the presence of these cage homes in a modern international city such as Hong Kong should not have existed at all. Yet, reports from the SAR government published in 2007 estimated that there were still 53,200 people living in such cage homes.

The then Hong Kong government did try to address this pressing issue. Thus it set up a statutory body called the Housing Authority, which is responsible for the administration of all issues related to housing. Its key objective is to provide and manage public rental housing (PRH) to low-income families who cannot afford private rental accommodation. As at end-September 2020, there were a staggering number of 156,400 general applications for PRH and about 103,600 non-elderly one-person applications under a quota and points system. The average waiting time for the general applications was 5.6 years, which many would regard as unacceptable. Clearly, the demand far exceeds supply and more needs to be done.

When I first arrived back in Hong Kong in 2012, despite the urging of some friends, I have never been tempted to buy any property for the simple reason that I could not afford it. If I sell my house in the UK, the price would be just about equal for me to buy a small 40 square metres flat in Hong Kong, perhaps third or fourth hand, in a high-rise block of more than 10 years in an ordinary residential area and without a car park. In Hong Kong, the average price of properties in 2020 is a hefty USD1.25 million, as mentioned in one of the earlier paragraphs in this chapter, which is more than the price of my house in the UK.

More Reclamation of Land

About two years ago, the SAR government did propose a hugely ambitious plan of reclaiming a vast part of Lantau Island into a residential area with the main aim of providing affordable housing. This concept is almost like building a city within a city. So far, this plan is long on ambition but short on details. No one knows the cost, which is guaranteed to be astronomical.

Furthermore, for this kind of massive infrastructure project, budgetary overshoots are always the norm, never the exception, on a scale not in millions but billions of Hong Kong dollars. No one knows the environmental effect and impact on the wild life habitat, which, once set in, cannot be undone. At best, the project at this stage can be regarded only as aspirational. In recent years, all major infrastructure programmes in Hong Kong always grossly overshot their budget, whether it was building a bridge or a new MTR line. The public, therefore, are naturally sceptical about the affordability of yet another massive, public purse string bursting project. Building a mini-city within a city is an undertaking which can potentially bankrupt both cities.

One other major possibility that is being actively considered, in addition to the Lantau Island reclamation project, is for Hong Kong to integrate further with southern China in a region around the Pearl River Delta called the Guangdong-Hong Kong-Macao Greater Bay Area (the Greater Bay Area). Covering nine cities in Guangdong province plus the Hong Kong and Macau special administrative regions, this is a much more far-sighted and ambitious project based on the integration and sharing of expertise and resources within a much bigger geographical area. It is a totally different project compared to the Lantau Island reclamation project, which is a new infrastructure starting from scratch with new land, new houses, and new transport system. The only attraction in this reclamation project is that the land so created, initially at least, will not be in the control of the property tycoons. But in my view, the Greater Bay Area is far more sensible as it involves pooling the resources from various cities to create a newer and bigger economically viable region, not a city. Besides, nearly all the infrastructure needs are already in place. This will be discussed in Chapter 11.

An Ageing Population

A rapidly ageing population is another pressing social and demographic problem that Hong Kong needs to face up to. According to the Census and Statistics Department estimates in 2013, the Hong Kong population was projected to increase to 8.38 million by mid-2033, representing a 25% increase over 20 years, with a continuous ageing trend.

The proportion of those aged 65 and over was projected to rise markedly from 11.7% in 2013 to 27% in 2033, with the median age of the population climbing from 38 in 2013 to 49 in 2033.

Currently, Hong Kong boasts the highest life expectancy compared with anywhere in the world, overtaking Japan and Switzerland, which traditionally occupied the top spot. According to United Nations figures, Hong Kong has claimed the top spot in life expectancy since 2018. More updated figures published by MacroTrends have confirmed that Hong Kong has continued to have the highest life expectancy in the world. In 1958, the year after I was brought to Hong Kong from Shanghai by my parents, the average life expectancy was 65.88 years and now by 2020, more than half a century later, it has increased to 84.89.

This high life expectancy clearly is a good thing in any society. We love our young and our old. There are many reasons for us to rejoice and celebrate having the longest life expectancy in the world. The key reason for this longevity is almost certainly the result of improvements in public health, nutrition and medical treatment for diseases. For this, Hong Kong people should be rightly proud. The people of Hong Kong enjoy good access to high standard medical care, both in the public and the private sectors. For the elderly, the geriatrics services in Hong Kong are not only well-developed, but are also well-integrated with other support services such as physiotherapy, rehabilitation, day care centres and community care homes. Also, the key provision of care to the elderly is not only treating the chronic diseases they may have but also providing support and rehabilitation in such an environment that the elderly feel safe, familiar and comfortable. In this respect, Hong Kong does indeed excel.

There are other reasons too. Companionship for the old is important. Unlike the younger ones, the elderly tend not to choose to live on their own or in nursing homes. In Hong Kong, many senior people live with their children, a shining example of the filial culture of the Chinese. My own mother, who is 96, lives with my brother and his family. That means old people are on the whole not only well looked after but also seldom lonely or ignored. In addition, alcohol or smoking related illnesses are rare among the elderly. The warm and wet weather in Hong Kong also helps as elders tend to be more vulnerable in the cold weather, and in Hong Kong they have plenty of sunshine for the production of vitamin D. Then there is the healthier diet. The Hong Kong Chinese diet tends to be based more on stir fried or steamed food rather than deep fried food with high salt and fat content. Boiled rice served with vegetables and fish is the popular staple food. This dietary habit is akin to the now fashionable Mediterranean diet. Chinese people as a whole are not too fond of high sugar content kind of food such as desserts, unlike the Westerners who not only have a fondness for desserts and sweets, but are also very fond of adding cream, sometimes even double cream, to their desserts. The net result is that elderly Chinese people in a warm place like Hong Kong tend to have less diet- related diseases.

So, good access to high standard integrated medical care, coupled with the traditional Chinese culture of caring for the elderly, climate and diets, all help to achieve the longevity of the Hong Kong people. Elderly people living on their own are very rare. Social deprivation and loneliness are usually not a problem.

Low Fertility Rate

Demographically, in looking at the ageing population, one also has to look at the fertility rate. To compound this ageing problem, Hong Kong has one of the lowest fertility rates in the modern world, with the most recent figure in 2018 showing a value of 1.1 according to the World Bank. The Hong Kong English language newspaper South China Morning Post reported in 2018 that the fertility rate in the HKSAR was at the bottom fourth in the world.

Yet this low fertility rate is not a result of poverty or even lack of access to high standard medical care. It is fashionable these days for young couples not to have any children or to simply choose to have one child only. This decrease in birth rate and an ageing population is bound to change significantly the demographic profile in Hong Kong within the next few decades, bringing with it all the social, health and economic problems that such changes in demographic profile would entail.

A fertility rate of 2.1 is the level at which a population can replace itself from one generation to the next. Studies conducted locally already have shown that the costs associated with housing, which was mentioned previously, and raising children, especially the outlay needed for a proper education, are the major factors deterring couples in Hong Kong from having children. In 2018, a survey conducted by the Hong Kong Women Development Association showed that more than 47% of the 813 Hong Kong respondents interviewed were not willing to have children, with housing being the top factor affecting their decision.

The low fertility rate, taken together with the fact that Hong Kong has the highest life expectancy in the world, does mean that the society will find it extremely difficult, if not impossible, not to burden the dwindling younger population to shoulder the cost and the responsibility of looking after the ever increasing old. Many commentators, sociologists and economists have already viewed this as one of the most challenging medium- to long-term socioeconomic problems faced by Hong Kong. The clock is ticking away.

In summary, the main social and economic challenges that the HKSAR is facing are housing shortages, income inequality, and a low fertility rate in a population which is rapidly ageing.

In the last two years, there is another huge problem related to the governance of Hong Kong and its future. This is the need for integrating the Hong Kong way of life with that of mainland China under the One Country Two Systems principle. How would this integration be achieved seamlessly with minimal tension? People in the HKSAR are used to living in a capitalist society with all the trappings and ills that come with a capitalist society while the mainland Chinese are used to living in a state-directed socialist society, albeit with some capitalistic elements, also with its trappings and ills of a different kind.

With all the big questions, politically, socially and economically, that need answering, I would like to make a prediction. I am convinced that the future of Hong Kong is best served by the integration of both systems, drawing on the successes and strengths from both systems, but under One Country. In order to achieve this, compromises need to be made by people from the existing two systems during this process of integration. This will be discussed in the next chapter.

CHAPTER 10
The Governance of HKSAR:
One Country, Two Systems

The future of Hong Kong was the main subject of Sino-British talks which started in September 1982 when the then British Prime Minister Mrs Margaret Thatcher visited China. Formal negotiations then followed afterwards with the direct involvement of the then paramount leader of China Mr Deng Xiaoping. A Joint Liaison Group was set up to conduct regular and intensive discussions on the future of Hong Kong.

The result of the discussions was the signing of the Sino-British Joint Declaration between the UK and China on Hong Kong in December 1984, which stated that Hong Kong would go back to China and would be under Chinese sovereignty. This Joint Declaration was then registered by the Chinese and British governments at the United Nations on June 12, 1985. According to the Joint Declaration, the Chinese government would resume to exercise its sovereignty over Hong Kong (which included Hong Kong Island, Kowloon and the New Territories, for which the land lease to the UK was to end in 1997). The British government declared that it would hand over Hong Kong to China on July 1, 1997.

It was also stated in this Joint Declaration that the governance of Hong Kong would be based on a One Country, Two Systems principle. The two systems being the socialist system as practised in China ruled by the Chinese Communist Party since 1949, and the capitalist system practised in Hong Kong during the colonial days under British rule. A Hong Kong Special Administrative Region (HKSAR) was to be set up under the authority of the People's Republic of China, and the historical governor of Hong Kong would be replaced by an elected Chief Executive, approved by the central government in Beijing on the basis of local elections held in Hong Kong. This election process mandates the electoral votes to an election committee of 1,200 members, with each voting member assigned to the great and the good in Hong Kong, representing the interests of various sectors of the local people.

Under this arrangement, starting from July 1, 1997, Hong Kong w ould enjoy a high degree of autonomy in running its own affairs except foreign and defence issues. The prevailing social and economic systems in Hong Kong would remain unchanged, and so would the life-style. Rights and freedoms, including those of the individual, of speech, of the press, of assembly, of association, of travel, of movement, of correspondence, of strike, of choice of occupation, of academic research and of religious belief would be ensured by the Basic Law in the HKSAR.

Private property, ownership of enterprises, legitimate right of inheritance and foreign investment would be protected by law.

The HKSAR would retain the status of a free port and a separate customs and excise territory. It can continue the free trade policy, including free movement of goods and capital.

The HKSAR would also remain its status as a financial centre with free flow of capital and the Hong Kong dollar would continue to be a freely convertible and tradable currency on the international capital markets. The HKSAR may authorize designated banks to issue or continue to issue Hong Kong currency under statutory authority.

These were the key parts of the Joint Declaration in which the Hong Kong way of life could be continued after the return of sovereignty over Hong Kong back to China.

To analyse these further, one needs to consider it from three different angles. Each of these angles has its own extremely valid reasons to ensure the success of the Joint Declaration and the smooth handover of Hong Kong to China.

First, for China, this was a historic event in the history of the People's Republic of China (PRC) under the rule of the Chinese Communist Party (CCP) that a territory, ceded to a foreign colonial power in one of the darkest periods in Chinese history (1842-1949), was to be peacefully returned to the motherland and sovereignty was to be regained by China over Hong Kong. This agreement happened at a critical moment as it was signed only a few years after the initiation of another historic event in China, which was its Reform and Opening Up policy. The timing of the agreement thus reassured and enabled Hong Kong to take full advantage of its proximity to China and its know-how in contributing to the reforms in China. By 2010, slightly more than 30 years after its launch, this Reform and Opening Up programme in China succeeded in lifting 600 million Chinese out of the United Nations' definition of poverty, which was a feat never before achieved in the recorded history of the world. Hong Kong, having enjoyed extraordinary economic success up to 1984, could continue to look forward to further economic success in the ensuing years. Its sovereignty would be rightfully regained by China, and its stability and prosperity could be maintained too. In achieving this, China could and indeed has capitalized on the expertise that Hong Kong could offer in playing a key part in contributing to the country's economic rejuvenation. So, as far as economic progress and national sovereignty are concerned, it was a win-win situation for China.

The return of Hong Kong to China was in the mind of the people on the mainland a powerful symbol of national renaissance, leading to the peaceful rise of China over the ensuing decades. Nothing caused national jubilation more than the return of Hong Kong to its motherland. This was not only deep in the mindset of the people in China, but also in the mindset of the vast majority of the people of Hong Kong too. The Joint Declaration, for lack of a better word, gave the people of both the mainland and Hong Kong a period to adapt to each other under the One Country, Two Systems principle. The people from both systems could learn from each other and augment each other's strengths. This Joint Declaration was celebrated nationally all over China, and in Tiananmen Square there was even a big clock counting down to the precise moment of the handover on July 1, 1997. By common consent, a historic wrong was righted, national humiliation was converted to national rejuvenation.

From the UK point of view, it had wanted to continue to govern Hong Kong as the country saw itself as making a huge success over the years in its administration of Hong Kong and played a direct role in the success of Hong Kong in gaining the reputation of being the Pearl of the Orient. If the UK were to continue its governing presence in Hong Kong, it could claim credit in the transformation of Hong Kong into an international hub of commerce, trading, banking, accountancy and transport, all of which were major successes and most were managed by British companies based in Hong Kong, such as the HSBC, Jardine Matheson, John Swire & Son (which owns the Hong Kong flag carrier Cathay Pacific). It could also use Hong Kong as a major springboard in participating in the Reform and Opening Up programme in China and achieve through this a major political and economic influence in its dealings with China. Simply put, the UK was very reluctant to give up such a pearl. In the end, it became very apparent that what China wanted and valued most was its sovereignty and territorial integrity, and the UK had to concede on that point. By signing this agreement, the UK might continue to foster a viable and ongoing diplomatic and economic relationship with China.

From the view of the Hong Kong people, this Declaration was important for some very different reasons. The people of Hong Kong with Chinese ethnicity were fully aware of the history of Hong Kong and how it became a British colony. They were also fully aware that colonial rule at some stage had to come to an end while accepting that Hong Kong was and should be part of China. This political reality was indisputable and unchallengeable. Yet, one has to recognize that a significant proportion of the people of Hong Kong were indeed immigrants from the mainland in the 1950s, 1960s and 1970s in search of a better life. These immigrants heard all about the successes and the glamour of Hong Kong. They wanted to be part of it, and they did become part of it. That was the reason why they came.

Before the Reform and Opening Up policy of China, there were various political movements in pursuit of political ideology, none more so radical as the Cultural Revolution which lasted 10 years from 1966 to 1976. The upheavals and the human sufferings it caused were incalculable in scale. This scarred the mindset of those immigrants from China who came to make a living in Hong Kong.

So, by the early 1980s, when the future of Hong Kong was first discussed between China and the UK, the people of Hong Kong were mainly concerned about the feasibility of continuation of their way of life. This way of life offered them great economic freedom and liberty based on a free market approach, leading to progressive prosperity. This liberty was accompanied by freedom of the press, of speech, and of expressions of opinions, administered by a civil service in a society free of corruption and protected by a reliable, fair and independent judiciary based on common law.

At the height of the negotiations between China and the UK, these concerns were so significant among the people of Hong Kong that there was, for a short period of time, a brain drain with a sizable emigration from Hong Kong to other countries like Canada, the USA, the UK and Australia. This brain drain, if not handled properly, could deter Hong Kong from further development, and fortunately, the brain drain did not last long and in fact many of these emigrants did come back to make a contribution to Hong Kong after things began to settle as the One Country, Two Systems principle provided an agreed framework to guarantee the Hong Kong way of life.

The Chinese government, in carrying out the negotiations with Britain, did understand fully the concerns of the Hong Kong people and the important role played by Hong Kong in commerce and trading, both internationally and with China. Indeed, when Governor MacLehose visited Mr Deng Xiaoping in 1979, the key message was that China intended to take back Hong Kong, but those investors in Hong Kong could put their mind at ease after 1997. In retrospect, this reassurance was powerful in its significance as it reassured the investors on the post-1997 scenario of Hong Kong.

If one considers the interests of the three parties above, then one can draw the conclusion that, in fact, the Joint Declaration did succeed in addressing these issues. Initially, many people in Hong Kong felt very unsettled and were sceptical about the actual implementation of the One Country, Two Systems principle as there was no precedent in the history books.

There was a crisis of confidence after the signing of the Sino-British Joint Declaration. It happened on June 4, 1989 when there were pro-democracy demonstrations by the students in Tiananmen Square in Beijing and on the day, the Chinese government had to deploy the People's Liberation Army (PLA) to quell the demonstrations, using armoured tanks in Tiananmen to clear the square and restore order. Lives were lost. There were no confirmed and validated records of fatalities, estimated from being a few hundred to a few thousand. The news was censored within China, but it did cause an international uproar and the people of Hong Kong were shaken and disturbed. There were for a while international sanctions against China. China defended itself by stating that this was an internal affair of no international impact and pledged that its Reform and Opening Up policy would proceed unabated. Looking back, this was seen mainly as an internal political event and although its impact on the economy of both China and Hong Kong was minimal, it cannot be denied that this might dent the confidence of the people of Hong Kong regarding the future.

After 1997, Hong Kong did experience three more difficult crises but not related to the Joint Declaration. The first was the Asian Financial Crisis in 1998, the second was the SARS (Severe Adult Respiratory Syndrome) crisis in 2003, and the third was the global financial crisis in 2008. Each of the three crises made a stutter in this engine of growth that is Hong Kong, but Hong Kong came through each of these crises pretty unscathed, not only with no long-term damage but actually economically stronger and more successful.

There are commonly held views among the people of Hong Kong that if one needs to assess the state of Hong Kong, one only needs to look at three indicators – the property prices, the stock market index, and the GDP growth in China. Since 1997, all three indicators have gone up significantly compared with the global average, while China has grown to become the second largest economy in the world as measured by GDP.

Of far more importance is the civil unrest after the handover. The first civil crack appeared in 2014. It started with the political movement initiated by some local politicians and academics over the way the election of the Chief Executive of Hong Kong is held. They wanted universal suffrage, in contrast to the existing system of representative electoral votes consisting of district representatives and functional constituencies (representing all the key sectors in Hong Kong such as medical, educational, recreation, banking, accountancy, retail etc). As a result, in August 2014, the key legislative authority in China, the Standing Committee of the National People's Congress (NPC) issued a decision regarding proposed reforms to the Hong Kong electoral system in which electoral reforms such as universal suffrage was subjected to prior vetting and approval of the candidates by the central government. This was not acceptable to the critics who had been advocating universal suffrage. They initiated a protest known as the Umbrella Movement as people used umbrellas to fend off tear gas. For a while, the movement occupied part of the key area right next to the SAR government building, close to the central business district in Hong Kong, causing significant traffic blocks and disruption. This lasted about 77 days. Things then started to recover and become normalized, but the seeds were sown for an underlying current of discontent and grievance.

The second crisis appeared in 2019. It was a governance crisis which directly threatens the survival of Hong Kong under the One Country, Two Systems principle. The triggering event, according to the Chief Executive of the HKSAR, Mrs Carrie Lam, was that a Hong Kong resident who was suspected of committing the murder of another Hong Kong resident in Taiwan had returned to Hong Kong. And since there was no existing extradition treaty between Hong Kong and Taiwan, the suspect could not be sent back to Taiwan for trial. Mrs Carrie Lam felt that this was a legal loophole which needed to be urgently closed. She came up with what was known as a new extradition law for the HKSAR, with the aim of closing the loophole. However, since at the same time, there was no extradition arrangement with mainland China either, this new policy might have much wider political implications and was viewed by some as a direct breach of the One Country, Two Systems principle.

This was because, by closing this loophole, it also implied that any Hong Kong resident who might have been suspected of wrongdoing in China could be sent back to the mainland for trial. This wrongdoing may not be criminal in nature, which is few and far between. More worryingly, would it mean unjust accusations of wrongdoings based on selfish business or even political motives? In other words, where there are differences in business practices between China and Hong Kong, would this extradition law lead to the using of unjust or unfounded accusations to get those residents in Hong Kong extradited and tried in a court in China?

Since the judiciary system in Hong Kong is independent under the Basic Law, therein lies the problem. The way the law is practised in Hong Kong is different from the way the law is practised in China. Even many prominent businessmen who had extensive business interests and experience in China, with proven track records of achievements, were concerned about this new extradition law. Although Mrs Lam did try to modify the proposed law to address these concerns, the alarm bell was raised. The concerns of the people of Hong Kong led to mass demonstrations over several weeks in June and July 2019, each with more than one million peaceful demonstrators. Hong Kong became the centre of attention in the international media and press. The protests were headline news everywhere. In the end, the proposal for the extradition law was withdrawn by the SAR government, but grievances and anger continued among some protesters. There were acts of violence and breach of public order. There were weeks and weeks of protests and confrontations between the protesters and police. People were arrested.

By May 2020, the civil order in Hong Kong was on the verge of a breakdown, and it led to the highest authority in China, the National People's Congress (NPC), to pass a national security law to be implemented in Hong Kong from July 2020. The enforcement of this national security law is to be directed and supervised by the setting up of a bureau run by senior security officials sent directly from China. The new law stated that all anti-government or anti-China protests or actions, or collusion with foreign countries or organizations will be illegal and thus liable to prosecution, and if convicted, will lead to a heavy prison sentence. Warrants for arrests can be issued for those who have sought asylum and protection abroad.

The introduction of this new law did succeed by the end of 2020 in stopping the protests in the streets. It has restored a semblance of peace to Hong Kong, even though Hong Kong, throughout the whole of 2020, was in the grip of the Covid-19 pandemic. Whether the newly introduced national security law will be able to once again rejuvenate Hong Kong as an economic power house is not clear. It will take years to pass a verdict. For the whole of 2020, and perhaps part of 2021, the SAR government had to devote all its energy to dealing with the Covid-19 pandemic.

CHAPTER 11
New Horizons in a Changing Landscape

Hong Kong at the Crossroads

Given what Hong Kong has gone through in 2019/20, how would events play out in the future?

Life is never plain sailing. There are always ups and downs. We can never guarantee or expect successes for ourselves as individuals. For a society like Hong Kong, it can even be very unpredictable, like sailing in uncharted water in an often turbulent sea. Stability cannot be taken for granted and assumed. It would be foolhardy to do so. There will be sunshine most days but equally, there may be dark clouds or storms, which can often shatter us. On the whole, if one remains steadfast, the storms will not destroy us. In fact, quite often, adversities and difficulties can strengthen us by bringing out our fortitude and our resilience. It can widen our scope of looking at things from a much wider perspective and as a result, the society we live in may be enriched or even enlightened.

This is one of the key reasons why I admire so much the people of Hong Kong who, though predominantly ethnic Chinese, live in a society with a wide variety of racial mix. Observers and commentators often fail to recognize or mention this. We have South Asians, Filipinos, the Gurkhas, British, Americans, Canadians, and Australians all living together in the melting pot in a land area of just over 1,000 square kilometres. The civic fabrics so created over the years are beyond nationalities. Everyone works hard, appreciates what we have and more importantly, appreciates others too, leading to mutual respect without resentment or prejudice. This rich blend of colours and backgrounds all combined over the decades to give us a civility that many other places in the modern world would admire.

People always comment, in passing, that Hong Kong people are smart and are only interested in making money. I think these people are completely missing the point, not to mention grossly simplistic in their view. They see what they see but sadly, fail to, or worse still, do not even try to, understand what they see. First and foremost, there is nothing wrong with being interested in making money. No one can be so morally superior in condemning others in the pursuit of higher profits or income through diligence and legal means.

A good example of this bias is illustrated by the acronym FILTH (Failed in London, Try Hong Kong). Many British expatriates, civil servants, businessmen, lawyers and senior business executives came to Hong Kong, settled here with their families and succeeded here in their own chosen careers. Yet their own people back home in the UK often came up with this somewhat sarcastic, even demeaning, acronym to describe their compatriots by using this patronizing and insulting remark on those who have made it here in Hong Kong. This does reflect a hint of lingering colonial superiority of an outdated mind, even though this empire has long gone.

The people of Hong Kong make Hong Kong unique not because they are smart in making money, but rather they are more industrious and resourceful to flourish in an environment which offers them freedom to act and to integrate with the rest of the world. It is the ingenuity and togetherness that make Hong Kong enjoy its economic success.

Even though the income inequality as measured by the Gini index is high compared with other places, there is, by and large, no resentment towards the rich in Hong Kong and in fact, the rich are more often admired. Civility and stability are helped by many charitable foundations mentioned in Chapter 8, of which the Jockey Club is by far the biggest contributor. The QUANGOs (quasi-autonomous non-governmental organizations), of which the Trade Development Council (TDC) mentioned previously is a classic example, also played a key and vital part in ensuring civility and prosperity in Hong Kong. All these organizations have contributed towards building a benevolent and progressive society, just like helping to provide the extra oil that greases the engine, or the sunshine and rain that make the flowers blossom.

However, this rosy picture has been tarnished in the last few years. There have been problems rising out of deep structural flaws in the fabrics of society. Cracks have appeared in the system and these cracks must be addressed before the system itself comes falling down.

First, as China becomes stronger and bigger, being now the second biggest economy in the world, the relative importance of Hong Kong to China is dwindling very fast, compared to the importance of China to Hong Kong. Even though Hong Kong still maintains its role as a major financial centre in Asia which helps to provide the financial know-how and channels that China needs, the overall influence of Hong Kong on China is much less now compared with the halcyon days when China first adopted the Reform and Opening Up policy.

In many other important sectors in this modern world, such as technology, bioinformatics, infrastructure developments, services industries, logistics, e-commerce, entertainment industries and pharmaceuticals, China has developed very fast and many cities in the mainland have already overtaken Hong Kong in these sectors. This is an almost inevitable result of the success of China over the last 40 years. In other words, Hong Kong is still prosperous but so is China, perhaps even much more so considering that the country has a population of 1.4 billion compared to Hong Kong, which has a population of 7.5 million. In addition, China has spent the last 40 years on making national efforts to lift its impoverished people out of the United Nations' definition of poverty and has successfully done so for

600 million people across the country, for which China has won international admiration as it was a feat never before achieved in human history. In this process, China has learned what works and what does not work. The expertise China has so acquired over the years in poverty alleviation will metamorphose into wealth creation. It is already widely projected that China may overtake the USA to become the biggest economy of the world in the next five to ten years.

While Hong Kong is striving to continue a model of minimal regulations and maximal commercial freedom to attract international banks and financial houses to consolidate its financial prowess, other important modern sectors may run the risk of bottoming out, or worse, hollowing out because of failure to compete, especially in the biotechnology, e-commerce and logistics sectors. Hong Kong may still have viable hospitality and tourism sectors, yet these are sectors that can least withstand external shock, as so clearly demonstrated by the Covid-19 pandemic. It is common sense for every household that whenever there is an economic downturn with an uncertain financial future, the first to be sacrificed is that spent on holidays while the essential household needs can be met by the convenience of e-commerce, without having to make a trip to the shops. The traditional retail industry is already in decline globally and in Hong Kong, this decline is already quite evident everywhere one cares to look. There are now more vacant shop outlets in the traditionally popular shopping malls or busy streets. Many shops are closed as income dwindles due to reduced sales, while rental cost has remained high. It is hard to see how these spaces can be converted to service viable businesses.

The only shop in the world which can defy this decline of shopping popularity is the Apple Store which, to this day, is possibly the only store with branches that are full of customers. But then Apple stores are full precisely because they are technology shops excelling in both the seamless integration of Apple hardware, software and mobile apps. In other words, it is a standard bearer of representing a new, sunrise industry.

The critics may therefore feel entitled to ask: apart from the current successful financial sector that Hong Kong has, is there any other alternative and forward-looking economic model which Hong Kong may adopt in the future? Is Hong Kong too reliant on its status of being a financial centre? Furthermore, this somewhat skewed success in the financial sector may even mean that for some people, mainly the speculators, the best and sure way to make money in Hong Kong is to play the stock market index and to buy and sell properties by dabbling in the property market. Both of these can lead to a bubble economy and asset price inflation can lead to a punch drunk effect on those on the make. For them, they only have to stay on the same track and their wealth will grow. This 'feel good' factor thus breeds complacency and lack of incentive to venture out into other areas. The unavoidable consequences of such a tendency are that entrepreneurship, innovation and skills in modern industry are overlooked, and therefore would not be given a chance to thrive and flourish. In the last few years, this has a particular unnerving and disturbing effect on the younger generation in Hong Kong. Unlike their counterparts in China, this despairing younger generation of Hong Kong now looks into their own future and finds that all is doom and gloom.

The despair the young feel about the future must be addressed, as these young people are in fact our future! Why are they in despair? One may ask.

First and foremost, they can hardly afford to live in their own accommodation, and this will probably deter them from having their own family, unless there is inherited wealth, or they have a fabulously well-paid job, which even in Hong Kong, is few and far between now. The net result is that they feel trapped, and they see unfairness and injustice all around them. While they enjoy the freedom that Hong Kong has offered them, they see no hope. There is a term which is not a new term for Hong Kong, it is a term called the millennials, first used in the USA, to describe the misgivings, resentment and anxiety of those aged between 20 and 35. I often do wonder if one of the reasons for the unrest in Hong Kong in 2019 may have something to do with the fact that Hong Kong has our own millennials who are filled with a similar feeling of resentment and grim prospect for a bleak future, since the vast majority of the protesters are of the same age as the millennials.

Most observers and commentators on the affairs of Hong Kong would have agreed that if there are any policy areas that the SAR government has not had the foresight to address in the last few decades, it would be the lack of a comprehensive, forward-looking youth policy and a housing policy. The SAR government has been too deeply entrenched, or indoctrinated, in the model of free market enterprise. While the SAR government is able to plan for and implement policies such as expanding public transport by having more tracks in the mass transit system, managing the medical services, and maintaining a pro-business environment, there is a lack of courage or will to tackle long-term structural problems. Far more importantly the SAR government must also have a vision to build a strategic long-term policy framework, including scoping and planning, to deal with not only the clear and present problems but also what Hong Kong needs in developing its future. Good governance is not only about effective administration and implementation of existing policies, but also about strategic thinking, even blue sky thinking, which is equally important.

It is a source of regret to me to note that every time there is a big debate on a possible major infrastructure policy, there is almost invariably a call to commission an international management consultancy company to advise on the feasibility of the policy. So a huge amount of public money is spent on reports by these consultancy companies, however well-intentioned and knowledgeable these companies are. Would these global companies, with their work committed all over the world, have enough local knowledge and expertise to advise us on a local long-term solution which suits our needs and addresses our problems? Are we not daring enough to engage in our own blue sky thinking? Extensive political discussion and consultation with the public will have to take place before the experts are asked or else the wrong answers will be given by the experts.

With all the major challenges lying ahead, there needs to be major changes on the horizon. The future may not necessarily be that gloomy. It would only be gloomy if we allow it to become gloomy. The younger generation in Hong Kong, whatever their resentment, does have an advantage and that is, they are well educated, judging by the ranking of our education system based on international standards. This is a major plus.

In the medium and long term, Hong Kong needs to look for areas for organic growth. In other words, Hong Kong needs to adopt a more expansionist economic and developmental model, and must not allow itself to be hollowed out by standing still, while clinging on to the misplaced and complacent notion that being one of the global financial centres, assisted by a tourism sector (most tourists in Hong Kong come from mainland China for a few days' stay only) and a retail sector would be the pinnacle of achievements. It was wrong to harbour these aspirations as the only things that matter and thus worth pursuing, without realizing that some of these aspirations, especially retailing, are already heading globally into decline, being gradually replaced by e-commerce and online shopping, even before the Covid-19 pandemic struck.

To adopt this expansionist model, Hong Kong must look beyond Hong Kong and not merely look into Hong Kong to see if it can maximize the collective skills and expertise acquired by its people in the last few decades.

If someone in Hong Kong looks east, they can see past the Pacific Ocean and reach the USA, Canada in the Northern Pacific and Australia in the Southern Pacific. If they look west, they can see the Middle East, Europe and then furthermost the UK and Ireland. But all these are faraway places which demand, even in the superfast modern day travel, the best part of a day, if not more. If they look south, they may see the many countries in South Asia and their rich cultural and religious mix. But if they look north, they can see China, which Hong Kong is part of, with a population of 1.4 billion people of the same heritage, and is now the second largest economy in the world and is predicted to be the biggest economy globally in the next five to ten years.

So, China is right on our doorstep, or more accurately, we are on the doorstep of China. The transport infrastructure (land, sea and air) setup is already up and running, including high-speed rail links to the rest of China and a major bridge in the Greater Bay Area. It is quicker for people in Hong Kong to get to the nearest city in China called Shenzhen than to go to a casino in Macau!

My own generation came to Hong Kong from China all those years ago in the 1950s. Now, given the transformative changes that China has undergone in the last 40 years, perhaps the time has come to think of moving back to China, in search of opportunities in exactly the way we did all those years ago. China is now a modern country and a big country. Is it not the right time for the independent minded, spirited and entrepreneurial younger generation to look north for endeavours in the new post Covid-19 world? Success is not guaranteed, of course, as it never is. But it is a very appealing, viable and sensible option. It certainly is more likely to be successful for the younger generation to start their own enterprise and seek affordable accommodation there than the present boxed-in situation where organic growth is hard to be generated from within Hong Kong.

The Greater Bay Area Plan

In February 2019, the State Council of China issued a landmark document which offers great opportunities for Hong Kong in the next few decades. This document is called the Outline Development Plan for the Guangdong-Hong Kong-Macao Greater Bay Area, known commonly now as the Greater Bay Area Plan.

This is a hugely ambitious, expansionist and far-sighted plan, setting out the blueprint for developments in the whole Pearl River Delta region in the next few decades. This Greater Bay Area project involves an area covering the southern part of one of the largest and most prosperous provinces in China called Guangdong, which boasts a population of 1.1 billion people. This is much higher than the 70 million population of the UK.

Essentially, the Greater Bay Area project links up Hong Kong, Macau and nine other cities in southern China, making it a regional geographical area comprising 11 cities, with three well-known modern cities playing a leading role each. These three cities are Guangzhou (the capital city of the province of Guangdong), Shenzhen (a modern metropolis of about 14 million population with a GDP higher than that of Hong Kong since 2018), and the HKSAR.

This project aims to foster economic growth in southern China by implementing an integrated economic and development plan across this area which would help China, already the world's second largest economy, to achieve further economic growth.

The blueprint for this plan focuses mainly on developing technology and innovation, boosting infrastructure expansion and increasing financial links between the cities. This area, based on the geography of the Pearl River Delta, will be a major hub not only for China, but for Asia too, servicing South Asia, Southeast Asia and Australasia. By common consent among the economists, Asia is forecasted to be the main global engine of growth in the next few decades.

This hub already has four international airports and three regional airports, four bridges, six intercity high-speed railway links and a modern road network. This delta region can also provide vital port facilities for outward and inward flow of goods through the South China Sea, thus acting as a true gateway to the world. The world's longest sea crossing bridge (55 kilometres) was built and completed already in 2018, connecting Hong Kong (a financial and commercial centre), Macau (a tourist centre) and Zhuhai (a city known for its liveability). Zhuhai is already regarded in the last few years by many as a good residential area to live in, and the logistics advantages offered by this bridge will be crucial in enhancing the expansion of affordable housing in all three cities.

Economically speaking, the Greater Bay Area is already very important to China. It is home to about 70 million people (slightly more than the whole of the UK), produces 37% of the country's exports, and accounts for 12% of its gross domestic product, according to HSBC research. The objective is that the closer integration of the region's cities can boost that economic growth and output further by synergizing services and developments, with freedom of movement of capital and investments, and a place to attract, train and retain a skilled and modern workforce.

In short, the Greater Bay Area project lays out the strategic visions for the major cities in this region of 70 million people to become the centres for trading, financial innovation, education, medical research, modern urban and eco-friendly designs, while providing plenty of affordable and modern housings for its residents.

In this blueprint, Hong Kong would strengthen its status as a financial and trading hub, and continue to play a leading role as a global centre of commerce, finance and banking. Shenzhen, home to Chinese telecoms giant Huawei and many others modern IT upstarts such as Tencent, would consolidate its position as a technology hub, while Macau would focus on tourism and trade with the Portuguese-speaking world. The role of the cities in this area will complement each other and not compete with each other. Other cities like Dongguan, which already has a very strong manufacturing base, can enhance the regional strength by becoming a modern manufacturing mega base with expertise in logistics and supply chains in the Greater Bay Area. By providing such a strategic development plan for this area and connectivity between these 11 cities, it is hoped that the economic output of the whole area in future will be more productive and bigger than the sum of its individual cities. This idea will not only make the whole region in south China competitive in trading with other countries in Southeast Asia, but also competitive with the rest of the world.

For Hong Kong, in particular, greater integration in the Greater Bay Area could boost its role as a global trade and financial centre. There are already some areas in the new modern sunrise industries which Hong Kong has fallen behind, such as bioinformatics, biotechnology, and modern logistics. The Greater Bay Area will offer Hong Kong a great chance to catch up and thus play a key part in these new industries. Nearby Shenzhen has already excelled in this field and so Hong Kong has much to collaborate with the expertise in Shenzhen to help the Greater Bay Area to reach a global level on these new sunrise industries. This project can also ease demand on Hong Kong's housing needs as it will encourage and make it more appealing for Hong Kong residents to move to the mainland, for both employment and residential reasons.

One very important area of this plan is that for integration to be implemented successfully, there would have to be a synchronization of mutually accredited and recognized professional standards. This would mean in practice that some professional qualifications can be applicable equally throughout the Greater Bay Area. Issues such as medical qualification, accounting qualification, educational qualification, and even aspects of legal qualification can be licensed within this area. This will need careful planning backed up by decisive actions in breaking down professional boundaries. It will be an important task as professional standards and qualifications tend to operate in a self-regulated closed system, unlike commerce and trade, which operate in an open system.

In my own experience, such cross-boundary professional recognition can be achieved, and I would like to share with the readers my own practical experience in this.

The University of Hong Kong Shenzhen Hospital (HKU SZH) was set up in Shenzhen in 2012 as a pilot hospital for medical reforms. The idea then was to introduce to Shenzhen the model of clinical practice and management expertise based in Hong Kong and in particular the Queen Mary Hospital, which is the premier teaching hospital affiliated to the Medical Faculty of the University of Hong Kong. I am one of the medical staff recruited from the UK by the University to take up a senior role at HKU SZH. In total, there are about 80 University staff crossing the border daily or weekly to go and work at HKU SZH. The group consists of medical staff, academic staff, nursing staff, pharmacists, accountants, therapists, imaging staff, physicists in radiotherapy, laboratory and managerial staff. All of us have the required professional qualifications accredited either in Hong Kong or overseas, such as the USA or the UK, related to our own field of expertise. But none of us have the equivalent qualifications in China. The Shenzhen municipal government, in its determination to introduce reforms, proceeded to give those of us employed by the University of Hong Kong a licence to practise in Shenzhen, renewable on a yearly basis, thus enabling us to work, along with our Chinese colleagues employed locally, at HKU SZH.

Now, some nine years later, this special arrangement has proved its worth. The professional boundary, as far as I can tell, among the professional groups between China and those from Hong Kong is hardly noticeable. As a practising haematologist, I do not feel any difference in me carrying out my clinical duties compared to my experience in the UK, nor do they feel any difference in working with someone like me who is from abroad. If I were to tell the young doctors who work with me and who do not know my background that I graduated in Shanghai 40 years ago and have never worked abroad, they probably would have believed me. For those of us from the HKSAR who work at HKU SZH, all we need to know is that this is our place of work where we ply our trade. As a team, mainlanders and those from Hong Kong should perform our duty to the best of our ability. I treat a patient with acute leukaemia in China in exactly the same way I treat the patients in the UK. More reassuringly, I can see this model of people from both backgrounds working together not only functioning well in the medical field, but also in other fields such as pharmacy, nursing and professions allied to medicine such as laboratory, radiology and therapy staff. In other words, this integration is across the board. Not only is it working out well for us, it is also worth pointing out that those of us who are not mainlanders are made to feel welcome by our mainland colleagues.

The success of the HKU SZH is particularly of significant relevance to the feasibility of the Greater Bay Area project as it is one of the clearest and most recent examples in demonstrating that professional boundary, important as it is in upholding standards, can be broken down to accommodate better integration of skilled personnel and widen the scope of developmental imperatives. Indeed, it has already been clearly stated in the policy blueprint that integration will be very important in areas such as accounting, medical services, education, teaching and academic research.

There is still much to do. The critics in Hong Kong are concerned that closer economic integration could be challenging for a region that includes cities such as Hong Kong and Macau which have different tax systems as compared to that of mainland China. The h ealthcare system is another classic example. It is fair to admit that these differences do exist due to the colonial past history of Hong Kong and Macau. It is also undeniable that the vast majority of the populations in both cities are ethnic Chinese. So any differences, though they exist, can be overcome since normally key barriers would be language and cultural, which do not exist under this plan. In coming up with this Greater Bay Area plan, the central government in Beijing would have held extensive consultations, discussions and internal debates before the plan was publicized as a national strategy in February 2019.

It is also my personal view that it is highly unlikely that the SAR government, or for that matter, the local governments within Guangdong or Macau, would have come up with any similar cross-border economic plan for this region on such a scale. This is not because of any suggestion of a lack of blue sky thinking on the part of the SAR government – it has to be understood that the remit of the SAR government is largely confined to Hong Kong under the One Country, Two Systems principle. The thinking and planning of such a major regional policy with such a far-reaching national economic impact and involving cross-border integration covering such a huge geographical area is only possible through the national directive from the central government in Beijing.

Actually, in the history of Hong Kong, both as a British colony and as a special administrative region of China, it has always served a distinct role for China as its window to the outside world, and in this process China was able to see how a traditional Western power such as the UK governed Hong Kong and in particular, how the free market system has worked in a city under the watchful eye of China. Hong Kong was actually the setting of many famous spy stories which I see as no bad thing, though the word spy seems to carry a meaning of being dark and clandestine. It would be nearer the truth, though, to say that Hong Kong, as the title of this book suggests, is an open society where East meets West, so information, know-how and cultural habits are more freely exchanged and learned.

Yet, until now, Hong Kong, even as a modern city, had never been considered as one of the key cogs in the wheel of such an ambitious and grand plan of China in which the HKSAR could play a key role in a region with a population of 70 million. Thus, this plan offers real opportunities for growth for Hong Kong, setting out a whole direction, backed by its own country, in a manner and on a scale unprecedented in the history of Hong Kong. The growth aspects will cover nearly all sectors in the economy, not only the financial and banking sector, but also education and research, especially since three leading universities in Hong Kong rank very high in the global league of universities. The experience that Hong Kong has built up over the years in urban planning, transport, and the provision of well-run public services can also be key areas where Hong Kong can contribute significantly to this plan. In making this Greater Bay Area a region of vibrancy and dynamism, there will be plenty of scope for the people in Hong Kong to play the vital role of key stakeholders. In addition, it will go a long way in solving the housing problem as it will for the first time provide a real alternative in seeking modern and attractive accommodation for those in Hong Kong who cannot afford the local sky high property or rental prices.

Nevertheless, there would be some people in Hong Kong who may be hesitant or sceptical about this major development plan, but I believe that this negativity will be temporary and short lived. Success breeds success and confidence breeds confidence. The views of the sceptics may come round once the plan goes from the drawing board stage to the implementation stage.

The people of Hong Kong must not let this opportunity slip by. History can be repeated. What the people of Hong Kong did in the last 50 years can be encored again. This time it is for the Pearl River Delta and for our future generation. What is needed for the plan to succeed is already in the DNA of the Hong Kong people – resourcefulness, adaptability, industriousness, far-sightedness, spirits of high hopes and adventurism. The success, when it comes, is not only for the working people, but for the children of the working people too.

It has already been mentioned in Chapter 9 that about two years ago, the SAR government was considering the idea of a massive reclamation plan for Lantau Island as a medium- to long-term solution for the housing problem in Hong Kong. Interestingly though, since the more ambitious Greater Bay Area plan was published, the advocates for the massive reclamation plan have all gone relatively quiet, although the SAR government was going ahead with a feasibility study. Certainly, in the public press and other discussion forums for policies, the Greater Bay Area received much more attention for the simple reason that this plan makes more sense in the long term not only in solving the housing problem, but also in raising Hong Kong to an even higher economic level. Simply put, the Greater Bay Area promises more potential and opportunities and is far less costly. The Greater Bay Area project's main thrust is on the connectivity and the enhancement of synergy among all the 11 cities, to consolidate a new economy built on the smokeless industries with added environmental merits. The Lantau Island reclamation project, for all its ambitions, is mainly an attempt by the SAR government to resolve primarily the housing problem for Hong Kong.

As with all ambitious and far-sighted plans, this Greater Bay Area project will need detailed and comprehensive planning. There will be an enormous amount of red tape or different regulations to be resolved in relation to transport, finance, banking, accounting, customs, immigration, and in some sectors such as the medical field, the need for mutual professional recognition and accreditation. The main objective is that for this integration to work, the red tape will need to be cut to the minimum to facilitate easier movement of people, goods and capital within the Greater Bay Area cities. The structure of governance in all these cities, be it public or private institutions, also needs to be established.

My own guess is that the initial five years will be mainly on planning and cutting red tape, attracting investment, infrastructure improvement and refinement. All these will need the participation of a workforce which is both skilled and experienced, a requirement which modern cities like Hong Kong, Shenzhen and Guangzhou are well-placed in providing.

There will be efforts spent on setting the right direction in exploring how various sectors can harmonize their regional differences. Such differences can be overcome by a determination and commitment to share mutual strengths. The success of the HKU SZH in Shenzhen mentioned above can be used as a case study on how integration can work.

Gradually, over time, the notion of One country, Two Systems will be of less and less practical importance. By 2047, the year in which the 50 years of the One Country, Two Systems principle will cease, the Greater Bay Area would have already turned the whole Pearl River Delta into a regional hub in Asia. It would be One Country. Hong Kong will still be able to retain its much loved nickname of Pearl of the Orient and will continue to occupy a prime and pivotal position in the regional and national economy.

On the point of cutting red tape, I would like to reiterate my personal experience with the readers. In 2012, I went to Shenzhen to work as a medical doctor in the then newly built Hong Kong University Shenzhen Hospital (HKU SZH) at the invitation of the University of Hong Kong. I am a graduate of HKU and still retain my medical licence in Hong Kong though I have worked in the UK for 32 years with a UK licence to practise too. I did not have a licence to practise medicine in China. Because my hospital is a collaborative project between the University of Hong Kong and the Shenzhen government, I was issued with an institutional licence to practise medicine in Shenzhen, upon production of my certificates of credential in Hong Kong and in the UK. I did not need to attend any examination. The granting of the licence has since been renewed on a yearly basis (same as Hong Kong) and since then, I have been able to devote myself, with no distractions, to working for the HKU SZH. I do not feel, as a doctor, any significant professional difference between working in Shenzhen and in the UK. So this successful integration in the field of medical practice suggests that there is no reason why similar collaboration and integration in professions other than medicine could not be equally possible and successful in the Greater Bay Area.

Though success cannot be guaranteed, the elements of success are being put in place already. So my own advice to the people of Hong Kong is that, in looking for opportunities, it is alright to look east or west, as it is the conventional way, but do not forget the new, exciting way by looking north, especially this north that is right on the doorstep of Hong Kong. On many occasions, some young people in Hong Kong and the UK would ask me about future career opportunities and my advice to them has always been: think north, think about the Great Bay Area, its aim and how you can play a role there!

CHAPTER 12
Hong Kong in the Post-Covid-19 World

This chapter discusses the specific impact of the Covid-19 pandemic on Hong Kong, with the hope that it can help to generate a debate on how Hong Kong can prepare for the post-Covid-19 world and further waves of outbreaks of such infection.

The world changed in 2020, as it is the first time the whole world has experienced a pandemic which hardly any living person has ever lived through before. The last pandemic, the Spanish flu, occurred just about 100 years ago, from 1918-1920.

The first documented outbreak of Covid-19 happened in the city of Wuhan in China in December 2019. On January 30, 2020, the WHO (World Health Organization) declared the Covid-19 outbreak as Public Health Emergency of International Concern. On March 11, 2020, the WHO confirmed the infection was caused by a virus belonging to the coronavirus families, and declared this Covid-19 infection a pandemic. This means every country or region in the world was affected.

By the end of 2020, this Covid-19 pandemic had reached a staggering 82 million infected cases globally and had claimed 1.7 million lives. No region in the world was spared. Most countries were caught unprepared, be it the governments or the public. Even for those countries which thought they were well-prepared, they were caught again with a second or third wave. This recurrent nature of waves of infection is, just like the seasonal flu, the very nature of a viral infection affecting the respiratory system. Some countries, like the UK, were going through their third wave by December 2020, and the third wave was more severe than the first two waves, due to the emergence of mutant coronavirus strains. Treatment and vaccine can help to protect us, and indeed, some very effective vaccines were already being rolled out by early 2021 with very encouraging early efficacy data, but they are unlikely to eradicate this disease, at least not in the near future. So, this virus will stay with us for some time. The WHO, in its 2020 end-of-year message to the world, has already stated that Covid-19 may be a fact of life in the future, either as a pandemic or more likely, an endemic.

This pandemic is a transformative event for all of us. It has taken lives and affected our livelihood. It also has had a profound and deep impact on the global economy, with an economic downturn even more severe than the global recession in the 1930s, following the 1929 Wall Street stock market crash.

Among all the debates and measures that have been taken to combat this pandemic, one thing that nearly everyone agrees is that we must protect ourselves by changing the way we behave and supporting the measures the society has to adapt as a whole to minimize the risk of present and future infection and transmission. Collectively, this is now known as the New Normal.

At the time of writing this manuscript, it was commonly accepted that Hong Kong had four waves of Covid-19 infections. Hong Kong had its first case in January 2020, leading to widespread public concern, anxiety and even panic buying when the supermarkets rapidly ran out of things like toilet rolls. This sort of panic also happened in the UK in March 2020 when Covid-19 first struck. Then, as in Hong Kong, the supermarkets in the UK also ran out of toilet rolls.

Despite all the panics in Hong Kong during the first attack, people by and large remained very cautious, as the painful experiences of SARS (Severe Acute Respiratory Syndrome) in 2003 were still very much fresh i n their minds. The relatively few Covid-19 cases were isolated quickly and cared for in the standard and purpose-built isolation wards with negative air pressure, which most Hong Kong government hospitals can provide. The public hospital services were not overwhelmed. Hong Kong did not have to enter into a lockdown mode. The public took the appropriate and necessary precautions such as the wearing of masks and social distancing.

Then the second wave occurred in Hong Kong in March 2020 when students studying overseas and residents living abroad started to return, leading to a spike in the case numbers. The

SAR government then instituted strict border control with China, even though by March the pandemic in China was beginning to recede. The SAR government also banned all overseas non-residents from entering its borders and every Hong Kong resident who did return had to have a Covid-19 test on arrival in Hong Kong and undergo a mandatory 14-day quarantine, with electronic bracelets in place to monitor the compliance of the quarantine.

These measures, in addition to the public willingness to comply with wearing masks and adhering to social distancing, were effective and for a few weeks Hong Kong did not have a single case of infection. The success of Hong Kong (with only five deaths up to June) has won international recognition and praise. Some members of the healthcare profession were even invited to give evidence at the UK Parliamentary Health and Social Care Committee in May 2020 on what areas of public health practices that the UK could learn from Hong Kong, as by that time the UK was going through the peak of the crisis.

Then the situation began to get worse. Hong Kong was struck by the third wave in July just when social restrictions were gradually eased. In the second half of the month, the number of confirmed cases began to climb to over 100 per day. In a period of 10 days, over 1,300 cases were identified, the death toll shot up to more than 40 and the public hospitals were at the point of being overwhelmed. The origin of the third wave was thought to be related to arrivals of untested and non-quarantined seamen coming to Hong Kong on commercial freights. Thus, further stringent measures were imposed by the SAR government. Health experts in China were asked to come to Hong Kong to provide extra technical support, especially on testing and screening for the virus for the public.

By August 2020, the spikes were starting to subside. The people of Hong Kong collectively also began to adapt to a New Normal way of life to protect themselves. This New Normal involves a whole repertoire of measures which need to be undertaken, some by governmental actions, some by changing of personal habits and behaviours, and some by collective civic actions.

But in October 2020, the fourth wave struck Hong Kong and this time it was not thought to have been imported, but rather it was thought to be related to an organised dancing group which recently had become a popular form of group activities where people can get together and have gentle exercises for about an hour. These were local outbreaks occurring almost certainly as a result that the virus has already seeded in the community, while the incidence of imported cases started to reduce. By the end of 2020, Hong Kong had a total of 8,611 cases with 137 deaths.

Vaccines for protection against Covid-19 have started to be produced in the USA, the UK, Germany and China and vaccination programmes have started in earnest in many parts of the world by early 2021. These vaccines do offer the global community a ray of hope but barely had vaccination started that British scientists identified a mutated strain of Covid-19 which has a higher transmissible rate though not necessarily leading to more severe infections or resistance to the vaccine.

Faced with all the rapid changes, it is even more important that one does not rely solely on the vaccine to protect us from the infection. We have to change the way we live and accept the need for a New Normal way of life.

Basically, there are two broad types of measures for dealing with the virus. One is pharmacological intervention such as vaccination, use of drugs such as antiviral, targeted antibodies or steroids. The other is non-pharmacological intervention (NPI) which means masks, PPEs, social distancing, change of behaviour and isolation. This NPI is the essence of the New Normal.

The New Normal is particularly important for Hong Kong in protecting itself from another wave. This is because Hong Kong basically covers a small area of just over 1,000 square kilometres, and its residential area is even smaller. Therefore, residential properties tend to be congregated in small areas with high-rise buildings (Hong Kong has always been known as a city of skyscrapers). For these buildings, there is no horizontal expansion for further space to provide for isolation as land is so expensive and very limited in supply, so only upward expansion is possible. Buildings of less than 20 floors high are generally rare. Thus Hong Kong has one of the highest densities of population per square kilometre in the world. Furthermore, for those less well-off people, they often have only a tiny area to live in, and as such, sanitation and cooking facilities cannot be expected to be adequate. Many of these high-rise buildings are at least 20 years old, and it is doubtful whether essential maintenance work such as drainage, piping and waste disposal systems are regularly carried out and updated.

Social Distancing and Isolation

Social distancing is well and good, and relatively easy to implement in an outdoor area and in public places, but at home, social distancing may be exceptionally difficult as there is simply not enough space for distancing. Imagine how difficult it can be for a young couple with a child living in a flat of barely 400 square feet. How would they practise social isolation if one of them has a fever or a cough? They would have no choice but to attend the hospital which would in turn put the other patients at risk. Furthermore, it is doubtful whether some of these high-rise buildings, especially those in the cheaper estates, would have an adequate ventilation system for fresh air.

Events in 2020 have proved without doubt that these oldish and high-rise estates are often where clusters of infections occurred. So these densely packed high-rise buildings collectively have provided a structural handicap, working against public health safety in any outbreak in Hong Kong. The way to resolve this is difficult, if not impossible, as property prices and rentals are so high. But still, the government has to recognize that this is an inherent risk for which at least there should be plans to institute measures to mitigate the risk, such as quick action of lockdown, isolation, rapid testing, together with meticulous contact tracing. This is what China has done successfully as it sets up a quick response task force with speedily enforceable actions.

Change in Culinary Habits

In dealing with the pandemic, there is another problem, which is arguably quite unique in Hong Kong. We, the Chinese, love our food. Our culinary expertise is world famous. Our sophistication and variety in matters of gustatory enjoyment have made a deep impression on the rest of the world. Not only do we love our food, but our food culture is also the main platform for socialization with families and friends.

Other cultures, such as those in the West, may have preferred afternoon tea or a pint of beer after work, but we prefer lunch and dinner. Tea or beer would be just the veneer of our socialization; lunch or dinner is the real thing. Not only that, we like to eat in a vibrant and lively environment. The more crowded the restaurants are, the more people will go there as crowdedness seems to imply popularity and value for money.

Because fondness for eating out is such an accepted and popular form of social engagement, Hong Kong has the highest concentration of densely packed eateries and restaurants in the world. One only needs to try the familiar sight, until the pandemic attack of Covid-19, of Sunday lunches in a crowded restaurant and see families of the young and the old all gathered together to have a family lunch. This is much like the traditional Sunday roast lunch in the West, except that in the West, lunch is usually served at home rather than a restaurant.

This eating out is part of our long cherished culture, and yet we have to realize and accept that even though this is what we cherish, it probably has to stop or at least be modified significantly especially in times of an outbreak. Crowdedness is the virus' best friend. My own mother, who is now at an advanced age of 96, has not been taken out for a public meal for more than one year (before the outbreak, she was taken out for a meal weekly). I think this is a price worth paying for, as safety comes first before anything else.

As a result, the SAR government, just like many other governments in the world, has rightly, in my view, banned mass gathering and imposed strict restrictions that no more than two people could eat together at the same table in the restaurants, which were only allowed to be open during the day, in times of outbreak. Many wedding banquets have had to be cancelled and even for those that are not cancelled, guests could only be allowed to sit at a table of four.

Another new normal, as far as eating is concerned, is instead of eating in eateries, one can start getting takeaway services. Online ordering and delivering of meals is already widely available and popular in China, where there is also a very efficient order and delivery service at an affordable extra charge. I worked and lived in Shenzhen for about 14 weeks over two periods in 2020, initially when Covid-19 was at its peak in China and then a second period when the crisis was under control. I witnessed and experienced first-hand how impressively efficient and versatile the system of online ordering of meals is. It was an eye opening experience for me. My colleagues could order breakfast, lunch and dinner simply by an app on their mobile phone. Often they ordered for me too. So Hong Kong may wish to copy this model and expand this order-and-delivery service. Even though the cost may be higher, it is still safer and much cheaper than looking after an infected person. The public may lose on the engaging ambience that eating out may offer, but if it can be traded off against better overall public health, then it would be a no brainer. The way we socialize by eating out in groups has to be significantly modified and furthermore, large group gatherings and banquets such as weddings, anniversaries and birthdays all need to be markedly curtailed.

Masks and Personal Hygiene

Our personal habits such as the wearing of masks or matters of personal hygiene will also need to be changed. On this, I feel confident that the people of Hong Kong will do well, given the painful experience that they went through during the SARS crisis in 2003. In Hong Kong, the wearing of masks in public is now the habitual norm. In fact, this is one area of good practice that countries in Asia such as China, Japan, Korea and Singapore can serve as a model for the rest of the world.

Another one is frequent hand washings in public, not only with soap and water but also with hand sanitizer gel. These sanitizers have to be readily available for use in the public places. All public places, such as restaurants, shopping malls, libraries, schools, airport, MTR stations, taxi stands, bus stops, lifts and elevators, have to provide these gels, on easy display for public use. These measures are not only effective, but also economically cheap to set up and maintain. They do not require a major capital investment nor do they require any software applications. Besides, they are not likely to be stolen or vandalized. The path to achieve this is straightforward and given the population density in Hong Kong in both residential and commercial properties, this may turn out to be another one of those universally accepted and effective measures.

One area which may deserve to be considered in this New Normal is, I would suggest, that the public should be encouraged to start to use handkerchiefs or flannels to dry their hands after washing. On this, many may see my view as not in keeping with the mainstream practice. We have all over the years been used to using tissue paper for drying our hands after washing or for other general purposes. Tissue paper is cheap, very light to carry around and disposable, but it is not recyclable or renewable.

Nowadays, we all try to be eco-friendly, but in times of a major outbreak like Covid-19, the demand for and the use of freely disposable tissue paper may be phenomenal. Heavy use will mean disposals of the used tissue paper may cause a major logistic problem, especially in public places. One must not forget that when the pandemic first broke out in early 2020, there were acute shortages of tissue paper and toilet rolls in many parts of the world. By solely relying on the use of such disposable paper in times of an outbreak, there may be a supply problem, leading to panic buying or hoarding.

The modern eco-friendly world is now emphasizing renewable and recyclable use of our resources, such as carbon-free energy, renewable or recyclable energy. Most of us would have noticed the rubbish collection bins these days are separated into the disposable or the recyclable. So for paper products such as used tissues, why not replace them with personal flannels which can be washed and reused again, with hardly any impact on the environment, while reducing and conserving our paper usage? We always use our own towels at home to dry ourselves after shower so why not encourage the public to carry a personal flannel, just like a personal mobile phone? This is a New Normal which should at least be considered, and the production cost will be less compared to the cost of producing and disposing ton after ton of tissues perpetually.

Since the SAR government has already been, in dealing with the coronavirus crisis, giving the public free facial protective masks, it would be reasonable to suggest that the government starts looking at ways to provide free and reusable flannels which can be washed. Such a move would be much better than providing cheap and disposable tissues for drying as disposal can be a logistical nightmare. The idea here is to offer an extra choice and not to replace disposable tissues altogether. After all, they both serve the function of a towel, except one is called a paper towel, which is disposable, while the other is made of washable fabrics to be used and reused personally. The cost of this would be less than providing free tissues on a massive and a recurrent scale.

I can imagine if I go to work via public transport with a mask and then suddenly I realize that I have forgotten to carry such a flannel with me in my backpack or pocket, I can go into any shop, such as 7-Eleven, to get a government provided small flannel for the rest of my day, instead of buying another pack of pocket size tissues, until I go home when this flannel can be washed and used again. There is no science needed in this. It is just a matter of common sense to enhance maximal convenience and compliance for all in the public in practising the same standard of hygiene. In addition, shops or eateries can even start to give out these flannels as freebies for the customers. In the age of the New Normal, a reusable flannel, perhaps even with the shop logo on for marketing purposes, would come in handy if we sneeze or wish to dry our hands. The key message to give out is that it is personal and reusable while it can also serve to enhance safety and reduce tons of used tissues for disposal.

Some would also advocate the use of a plastic facial shield for protection. This is of course another safety measure, but it can only be best used by workers in stationary jobs such as cashiers in a supermarket but not for those who move around or travel in public transport, as these shields can cause problems purely because of their size.

One of the distinguishing and almost unavoidable events in a day in the life of a Hong Kong resident is using the often congested Mass Transit Railway (the subway system in Hong Kong abbreviated as the MTR). Just like other similar systems in London, New York, Beijing and Tokyo, it is always congested with people squeezing against each other during the rush hours as its capacity was never designed to cope with such high numbers of passengers. In the morning, people rush to work and to school. In the evening or at the weekend, people go out socializing with their friends.

In any underground transport system, movement from A to B is relatively easy and convenient. Yet, during a crisis like Covid-19, this efficiency and the congestion will invariably be a major public health hazard in the control of droplet infections. It is now universally agreed that in times of an outbreak such as Covid-19, one of the most effective personal measures that one can take would be social distancing. In Europe and the UK, the recommendation is a distance of 1.5 metres to 2 metres between two individuals. This requirement of social distancing in a transport system like the busy MTR underground network in Hong Kong is impossible to implement at peak hours. It simply is not physically possible.

In dealing with the pandemic caused by droplet infection, public health and safety are much more important, and therefore should take priority over the speed and convenience in travelling in the MTR. Take for example the supermarkets in the UK around Christmas time in 2020, when the country was facing the high infection rate of a more transmissible virus which has mutated and identified by the UK scientists to be a new variant. In the supermarkets in the UK at the peak time of the crisis, even at Christmas, people were willingly keeping a safe distance from one another. Everybody was waiting patiently in the queue. This orderly behaviour of social distancing has been in place since March 2020 in the UK. Gone are the days when there were clear signs of rush and impatience in these lines. There is every reason that the same should be encouraged in Hong Kong, but, it can be fraught with difficulties. The people of Hong Kong are known for their demand for efficiency and every task is measured by the speed in which the task is completed. But when it comes to the Covid-19 pandemic, it is a public health matter where everyone needs to be compliant with social distancing. The speed of the task pales into insignificance when it comes to public safety. And, for the use of public transport such as the MTR, how could one deal with the peak hours of congestion? It is nearly impossible unless the city is in a lockdown mode, in which case everyone is staying at home, venturing out is kept to a minimum and there will not be passenger congestions in the MTR.

Working from Home

One of the ways currently under discussion to reduce congestion is if the New Normal can encourage more people to adopt the practice of working from home in order to reduce cross infection in the congested public transport system. In Hong Kong, this merits particular consideration as it is inadvisable and impractical to deter people from using the MTR by suggesting to the public to use alternative forms of public transport such as buses, minibuses or taxis, as the MTR provides the main routes connecting various parts of Hong Kong. Other forms of transport are there to supplement the MTR, not to replace it. Since the road traffics are already congested by buses, lorries and private cars, there is no capacity for more cars on the road.

By encouraging people to work from home, there is of course the natural concern that if people are not seen to be working in an office with others, then people are likely to put in less effort when they are at home, where there is no supervision by peers. This theoretical concern over productivity and human behaviour is the main reason why institutions are not willing to encourage working from home. But in truth, up to now, there is no proof to show that productivity is lost as a result of working from home. The banking industry has already carried out surveys and published studies that found productivity was not shown to be lower when the banking staff work from home.

The SAR government has already successfully asked its civil servants to work from home during the peak of the crisis. Therefore, it is a matter of proper planning and the government can take the lead by being more proactive in exploring this on a semi-permanent basis. For instance, it can assess if the office hours of the civil service can be redefined in such a way as to help reduce the pressure of congestion the MTR has in the peak hours. The civil service in Hong Kong numbers around 180,000 people. It is not a small number, nor is it a big number either. Given that the total number of people at work in Hong Kong was estimated to be around 3.85 million in 2019, and that not all of them worked the nine to five office hours, it is entirely possible for the SAR government to assess how the working hours of its civil service can be modified. One very viable option is for the government to explore whether the civil service can work three days in the office and two days at home on a rotational basis. This could possibly help to relieve significantly the passenger congestion in the public transport system during the peak hours. It is worth considering, at least as a pilot project, at the outset of any future wave of infection outbreak.

Most retail shops, especially those in the shopping malls in Hong Kong, already have opening hours starting either 10 am or 11 am while most eateries serving breakfast have a much earlier starting time. So it is not in the realms of impossible that the SAR government can start to consider staggering and rotating the office hours. For instance, the younger, childless ones could start at 8am and finish at 4pm, while those with children could start at 10am after dropping their children at school and finish at 6pm. Alternatively, the civil service could also consider the idea of either changing the office hours by a longer working day (say 8am - 8pm) for three days a week. The net result is that both the MTR would service fewer people while the offices would be less crowded with workers, which is better for social distancing. This can be especially applicable to the rank and file staff.

The clear evidence as to why this should be considered is that on public holidays, the MTR is not as congested in the rush hours as a normal working day. Schools or bank closures may be a factor on public holidays but equally the absence of civil servants going to work is also a major factor.

In this particular area, of major relevance to Hong Kong, being an international financial centre, is the report of a survey carried out by the US investment bank Morgan Stanley and published in August 2020 in The Sunday Times in the UK. The survey showed that almost three quarters of accountancy, banking and finance workers would prefer to work from home, especially among the younger workers, as it leads to better balance of work with domestic needs, while there is no evidence that productivity is affected. Answering a phone query or replying to an email from a client or customer can just be done at home as the technology is fully mature here. In addition, professional meetings can be conducted at a predetermined time through video conferencing such as Zoom. This survey about social trends in the pandemic of 2020 is food for thought indeed. In this age, especially when the internet connectivity is so fast, reliable and efficient, there is every reason to be positive about this working from home concept. In addition, any meetings or emails of work over the computer or any mobile electronic device such as a modern smartphone can be recorded and digitalized as a record. Government can take the lead in developing this, so there is every chance that the next wave can thus be contained more efficiently and speedily.

The Use of Telemedicine

Hong Kong also has an ageing population, as previously mentioned in Chapter 8. It is self-evident that the elderly and the frail would be in the high risk group to catch the infection. This would mean they need to be prioritised to receive any medical care and attention they need during the pandemic. It has to be pointed out that the elderly, when they seek medical attention, are usually accompanied by their family members or a maid, regardless of whether they seek the medial attention in the public or private sector. Each consultation will involve a back and forth journey of almost certainly a time span of at least four hours, including the waiting time in the clinic. This is where the New Normal can come in to help, by linking the patient, the family members and the healthcare professionals via the practice of telemedicine. The practice of telemedicine is already very advanced in China. I use telemedicine on a regular basis in my practice and now the UK is also fast catching up since the Covid-19 pandemic.

The providers of healthcare in Hong Kong, by that I mean the doctors, the nurses, the therapists and the pharmacists, are all, without exception, very techno savvy. It would therefore be very useful if they can be encouraged or even mandated to carry out their consultation via telemedicine, and the record of the consultation can be digitalized and stored. Most medical consultations these days, unlike the past, do not require physical examination of the patients, as modern diagnostics are so accurate and advanced. In Hong Kong, on occasions, because of clinical needs, a patient such as those receiving chemotherapy or treatment for diabetes, a blood test is needed prior to their consultation, so the doctor can have the most up-to-date information to make an effective clinical decision. In the new age of telemedicine, this practice can even be enhanced as the blood test can be done via the local health centres, and the results can be checked electronically both by the patient and the doctor prior to the appointment time, as is already happening in China.

I personally do not have the data of how many specialist outpatient appointments are provided by the public hospitals in Hong Kong on a daily basis, but I would conservatively guess that around 70% of these are follow-up consultations (those whose primary diagnosis has already been established in the specialist clinics) and some of these chronic cases can be safely moved over to telemedicine. There would be no travelling time required for the patients and their family members, and most importantly, they can be protected from possible cross- infection in the clinic. It is never a good sign that hospital outpatient departments are overcrowded and patients are kept waiting. The introduction of and the more widespread use of telemedicine will therefore be a very powerful and effective tool in infection control, in addition to the improvement in patient care.

By the same token, the practitioners in the private sector in Hong Kong can also consider such an alternative way of providing professional opinions, especially since clinics of these specialists in the private sector always tend to be located in densely populated buildings in densely populated areas. The antagonists against telemedicine like to point out that the patients like to see their doctors. Telemedicine is designed so that patients do in fact see their doctors, and it would not be a masked face to masked face consultation, as it is now currently the case in the clinic. In fact, certainly in the public hospitals, it is often the case that the patients get to see a different doctor of the same specialty every time they go to the clinic anyway. The only way that the patients can get to see the same doctor of their choice in most places, such as China, the UK and the USA, is when the patients choose to see the doctor in the private sector. Telemedicine practised in this way would be far more productive and safer for the providers (the doctors), the users (the patients), and the intermediaries (the families or the maids).

In my own experience, I have not needed to see my General Practitioner (GP) in the UK since the beginning of 2020, but I have on four separate occasions used telemedicine to get the appropriate attention that I needed from the GP practice. It is effective, safe and convenient for me, and the same for the GP. Their time can be freed up to attend to those who really need to see them in a less crowded clinical environment. Hong Kong must really start to look at this. It has been proven to work with no compromise on patient safety, both in China and the UK. If a prescription is needed, it can be electronically issued and collected at a convenient time by a family member in the public hospital or better still, in a designated pharmacy. Some UK pharmacists actually offer delivery of medicine to patients' homes.

Videoconferencing

Following on with the use of telemedicine, the same can be said of professional conferences or managerial meetings. These days, the New Normal has introduced to all of us a new tool called Zoom and now nearly everyone knows about Zoom. This is how we connect with our friends and business contacts and how the politicians and civic leaders conduct meetings themselves in the age of social distancing. So equally, it should be a matter of policy that teleconference could be prioritized over face-to-face conference where everyone from different departments and offices all congregate in one room in which all the individuals must engage in collective precautions that such face-to-face meetings entail. For a modern metropolis like Hong Kong, I can see no difficulty in adapting to this New Normal. Hong Kong has always prided itself on being at the forefront in the use and application of technology. This will be a change tailor-made for Hong Kong, made all the more relevant as it enables the professionals to maintain contact with the outside world, be it Greater China, the US, Europe or anywhere else. Since international aviation is markedly curtailed, the senior executives would probably breathe a sigh of relief for not having to suffer from the jet lag from frequent flying. Instead, these senior executives can conduct their business in the comfort of their own home or office.

On this particular point, it is interesting to point out that there was a US Congressional hearing in July 2020 where the CEOs of the Big Four, namely Amazon, Facebook, Google and Apple, were asked to give their views at this hearing. All the news channels in the US were expecting to cover the CEO testimony of this Big Four in the US Congress. The big network TV all expected it to be a top box office hit with high viewing figures, but then when the meeting did occur, the CEOs all gave their views via teleconferencing. Even though it turned out that this was no box office hit, since the superstars did not make an appearance, the relevance of this congressional hearing was not affected. The congressional leaders were still able to ask their questions and the CEOs were able to provide their answers. I would guess on that day, the Congress would be less crowded than anticipated and so the real purpose of the meeting was better served. There were no dramas to cloud the issues and yet the hearing was still broadcasted live. Questions got asked, answers were given and proper transcriptions recorded and kept. There was no fuss, no stage acting, no grandstanding either.

The use of streaming technology can have other areas of practical application too and that is on education, especially tertiary education. This is already accepted as one of the main tools globally on how tertiary education or even secondary education can be delivered. One area of controversy on this is that in countries like the USA or the UK, where most tertiary institutions charge significant tuition fees for overseas students (the fees can be as high as half a million Hong Kong dollars per year), there is a feeling that such tele-education does not give the students value for money. In Hong Kong, this may be less of a problem as nearly all the tertiary education institutions primarily cater for the needs of local Hong Kong students, with much fewer overseas fee-paying students compared to the USA or the UK. This form of tele-education is much more flexible for the teaching staff. Even overseas or guest lectures can be arranged this way for the students. There is at present no evidence to suggest the standards of education will drop. As far as I know, there is no survey to date suggesting that the students prefer face-to-face lectures more. Again, just like the suggestion of using reusable and personal flannels, this is to widen the formats of a lecture. To give a lecture in a lecture hall, one has to ensure that students may have to sit apart from each other and may even have to declare, before they attend, if they have a fever prior to their attendance or have their travelling history checked! For me, I started to give weekly tele-teaching sessions or tutorials to the young residents in the hospital I work in in China since March 2020, and it has been well-received since.

Capacity Constraint

One final but important area which must be addressed, specifically to Hong Kong, in this discussion of coming to terms with the New Normal is when, how and where from, if Hong Kong does need outside assistance. Hong Kong, even as a modern city, cannot expect or be expected to be self-sufficient in everything. There are constraints everywhere. To think Hong Kong can handle most things is an irresponsible and even dangerously arrogant attitude to take. In times of crisis, not only do we need sound advice and effective action, we also need outside help. Arrogance and complacency is an invisible and self-created hurdle at times of crisis.

This question has been laid bare in July 2020, when the public hospital system and the private laboratories in Hong Kong were on the verge of being overwhelmed by the onset of the third wave of infections. Even the participation of the private hospitals could not provide the spare capacity of the medical services that Hong Kong needed. Operations had to be cancelled. One of the key reasons why Hong Kong was woefully caught ill-prepared was its limited testing, tracing and diagnostic capacities in such a crisis. In other words, the testing capacity in any public health outbreak has to be expanded many folds as not only the suspected cases need to be tested, but all the contacts of confirmed cases need to be tested too. In July 2020, Hong Kong was faced with the shortages and constraints in having the necessary laboratory equipment, reagents and the technical staff to carry out these tests. So the overall ability to control the infections outbreak was hampered by these constraints. There were also inadequate isolation beds. Such inadequacies could be a real danger to the public, as it meant the crisis could not be properly handled and transmissions could go unchecked and untraced. To be fair, this was not a problem that only Hong Kong faced. Nearly all countries were caught short. In the UK, the testing capacity was so restricted that the epidemiologists and the scientific advisors to the UK government had to make all the modelling and projections on how the pandemic would turn out based on limited testing data; it made grim reading. The testing capacity in the UK only reached a far more acceptable level after nine months, by December 2020. This only happened after extra resources were put in to upscale and upgrade the testing capacity of the laboratories.

In early August 2020, the SAR government asked the central government in Beijing for help and as a result, the central government arranged a team of medical, nursing and technical staff, most of whom were able to speak Cantonese as well, to come to the aid of Hong Kong. The task of the team was mainly to vastly increase the testing capacity in Hong Kong. Experience in the preceding seven months in China and elsewhere had shown that early isolation, extensive testing and contact tracing are the keys to containment of the viral outbreak. China has unique experience and capacity in such testing. Since China was the first in the world to identify the RNA make-up of the Covid-19 virus, China is equally well-placed to produce its own reagents to meet the testing demands domestically. Not only that, China has already launched a national effort of testing and tracing of Covid-19 since January 2020. This has helped China to acquire rapidly the expertise needed to produce the test kits and reagents as well as enhancing the technical know-how of the laboratory staff in performing such a test with a fast turnaround time. In my own hospital, the HKU SZH, the turnaround time is six hours and testing is a 24/7 service. In short, China now has a successful and effective test and trace policy. This is why China was able to assemble a team of experts in such a short time to come to Hong Kong to help in an area which Hong Kong was acutely in need of.

I think this was an appropriate and necessary move. This was a real test of the One Country, Two Systems principle. Nowhere has it ever been stated that one system can exist at the exclusion of the other system under One Country. Regrettably, there was some antipathy shown towards the team of experts arriving in Hong Kong. This antipathy was primarily concerned with the fact that the professional qualifications of the team are not recognized in Hong Kong and thus quality and standards might be different from that required in Hong Kong. Implicit in this antipathy is an underlying display of unfounded assumptions, arrogance and prejudice about the technical expertise and competence of the team from China, even though members of the team were all hand-picked in the country for their know-how and experience. Regrettably, only 1.8 million people in Hong Kong showed up for testing.

But extraordinary times would need extraordinary measures. The public health safety of the Hong Kong people was at stake and control of the third wave was the top priority, especially when the healthcare system could not cope. So the other area that this team from China was tasked with was to advise and manage the temporary makeshift hospitals which would provide the single purpose extra beds that Hong Kong desperately needed for the infected patients. These extra makeshift hospitals are now the standard in many countries, they serve the dual functions of looking after the Covid-19 positive patients and separating them from the non- Covid-19 patients. In the UK, these hospitals are called Nightingale Hospitals as the layout is similar to the concept of the original Nightingale ward which was an open ward with work stations with the medical and nursing staff in the central area.

Given the unique situation in Hong Kong, where the population density is high and living space for an average family is limited, together with the unpredictable nature of the next wave of infection, the presence of such a step-up option of extra hospital beds with extra staff of relevant experience is reassuring to the public and the government. Prejudice and tribal thinking must be put aside for the common good, especially since it is usually the helpless and the voiceless that need our help most. Where there are areas in dealing with the pandemic in which Hong Kong finds itself short, especially in areas where China is doing much better, such as isolation, partial or local lockdown, test and trace, diagnostic capacity and supplies of vaccines, then the SAR government should turn to China for advice and assistance, and the public should support it.

CHAPTER 13
Hong Kong or Shenzhen – How do I choose?

I am a Hong Kong citizen and have spent more than 20 years in Hong Kong, where I received all my education. In later years I worked in the UK for about 32 years. Now I have gone full circle, having lived and worked in Shenzhen and Hong Kong in the last nine years. During my 32 years of working in the UK, I visited Hong Kong on a regular basis, about once or twice a year, to see families and friends. For a previous resident of Hong Kong like me, it is hard to resist the sentiment and the urge to come back on a regular basis, either by myself or with my wife and son.

In making such frequent visits to Hong Kong, it was manifestly difficult not to have the feelings that Hong Kong is constantly changing and always seems to be on the upward trajectory. This has never failed to impress me. There has always been a very distinctive air of vibrancy and dynamism about this place. Every time I arrive at the airport for entry into Hong Kong, I have that unavoidable uplifting of spirits, developed over the years, that one can only feel but would find it hard to describe.

Now, I have also worked and lived in Shenzhen in the last nine years. I once visited the local Shenzhen Museum in which a motto was displayed, which is translated as: Now that you have come to Shenzhen, you are a Shenzhen-er! This is as welcoming a message as it can be. I was deeply impressed when I saw it. The words were carved out in classical Chinese calligraphy style.

People always ask me, in view of my own experience of having gone through the full circle, from being born in Shanghai, then moving to Hong Kong, then to the UK, then back to Shenzhen in China in a span covering more than 60 years, which city do I prefer? By that they always mean Hong Kong or Shenzhen. This is a question to which an answer can be either very easy, by saying I like both cities, or difficult, by saying neither! I shall try to explain my views here.

For a start, both cities are very modern, with a distinctive vibrancy and liveliness that one gets to feel about any modern metropolis. Visually, both cities are staked with modern, high-rise buildings. Both have made remarkable progress in the last 40 years and in fact, Shenzhen's achievement is even more groundbreaking, considering that it was a little known local fishing village of about 60,000 people some 40 years ago while Hong Kong then already had a population of about 3.5 million people. Hong Kong was much more modern then. In those days, Shenzhen as a village had no modern roads and cars were nowhere to be seen. Now, traffic jams are the norm in both cities during peak hours.

The current population of Hong Kong is about 7.5 million while the Shenzhen population is estimated at about 14 million (there are many unregistered migrants with no local resident status. In China, this resident status is called *hukou*). The population profile in Shenzhen tends to be younger (the average age is 32) and its GDP has overtaken that of Hong Kong since 2018.

Because of the proximity of Shenzhen to Hong Kong (travelling time from the commercial centre in Hong Kong to the commercial centre in Shenzhen now takes approximately 35 minutes, the shortest time between any two major international cities in the world), the economic development model undertaken by Shenzhen was very similar to that of Hong Kong in the 1960s and 1970s. It started off with a low-cost manufacturing industry with a labour force provided by the inflow of migrants from the rest of China. These low-paid hardworking people made an indelible mark on the success of Shenzhen. The city then gradually climbed up the value chain to make high-end products and in recent years, Shenzhen has successfully developed a high-tech sector for its economy. While Hong Kong has now excelled as an international financial centre, Shenzhen has now excelled as a technology centre, and is home to some major techno giants in China.

For me, I see and appreciate the attractions that both cities can offer, especially if one's preference is to have a sense of modernity in urban living. The Lonely Planet Guide in fact listed

Shenzhen as the second most desirable city to visit in 2019 after Copenhagen. Modernity was cited as one of the main reasons for the recommendations by Lonely Planet. Hong Kong perhaps is more scenic as it has the harbour, the sea, the islands and the mountains. Shenzhen has the Shenzhen Bay offering a scenic view across to the northern part of Hong Kong with a beautiful bridge linking the two. The public transport systems in both cities are very efficient and convenient though for personal and selfish reasons, I slightly prefer the Shenzhen system more as it offers a free ride to those aged over 60 while the Hong Kong system charges a flat concession rate of HKD 2 per journey! For taxi journeys, I prefer the Shenzhen system also. This is purely for the simple reason that nearly 100% of the taxis in Shenzhen are electric cars which are more comfortable and quieter. I don't normally get much time to travel on the bus but if available, then I would prefer the bus in Hong Kong because the routes that the buses drive past are more scenic, especially from the upper deck, while Shenzhen does not have double decker buses.

Living conditions in Shenzhen are also remarkably similar to Hong Kong. This is possibly because over the years, the municipal government in Shenzhen has developed a knack of urban planning, based on the experience it has accumulated over the years by studying how other cities such as Beijing, Shanghai and Hong Kong carry out their urban planning. There are many high-rise buildings clustered together like housing estates, with essential amenities like shopping, supermarket and children's playground available in each estate, thus establishing a self-sufficient community of residents, well-served by public transport. I witnessed at first-hand how, at the height of the Covid-19 outbreak in China in February and March 2020, the local estate or community played a vital role in the implementation of the lockdown when the residents in each community were checked and monitored individually for their movements and how daily essentials were provided for the local residents.

When it comes to the comparison of the cost of living, then on average the cost of living is undoubtedly significantly lower in Shenzhen. Various estimates have been put forward and on the whole, it is about 35% cheaper in Shenzhen. Even though the property prices and the rental costs in Shenzhen have become higher in recent years, they are still lower than Hong Kong.

For the relatively well-off, Hong Kong has a significant advantage in that it has legislation which allows its residents to employ imported, live-in maids, called domestic helpers. These maids were originally from the Philippines, but this scheme has now become so essential and popular that this market has been expanded to include the recruitment of domestic helpers from Indonesia and Thailand as well. So there is a certain degree of home comfort and even luxury, which the average families in Hong Kong enjoy but which Shenzhen families do not have, since imported labour as domestic helpers is not allowed. Employing domestic helpers in China is generally more costly and difficult, so the average family relies mainly on their parents for domestic help. For those families in Hong Kong which do not need or could not afford to have domestic help, then there is minimal difference between Hong Kong and Shenzhen, except Shenzhen on the whole is cheaper.

Another important area which we always consider is the quality of our culinary experience. This is part of our cultural trait developed throughout the thousands of years of Chinese civilization. If two Chinese are engaged in buying a property to live in, be it in China or elsewhere, one topic which always comes up is the availability and the quality of the Chinese food in the locality. Such a topic would not have entered the mind of say, two British, if the same topic of buying a property comes up.

In fact, the word Chinatown used all over the world refers mainly to a constellation of Chinese restaurants or eateries, all serving different kinds of Chinese food within a small and somewhat ill-suited neighbourhood. These Chinatowns will always have some Chinese supermarkets as well, selling ingredients essential for Chinese cooking, which are otherwise not available anywhere else.

In Hong Kong, the Chinese food is very good and not only that, there is also a wider variety of international cuisines on offer such as Italian, French, Indian, Japanese, Thai and Korean food. On the whole, these are more expensive. In Shenzhen, there is less of an international variety compared with Hong Kong, but Shenzhen offers something else which Hong Kong so far could not. Shenzhen offers different regional cuisines from all over China. The variety on offer is jaw-dropping. If one goes to a shopping mall in Shenzhen, one would invariably encounter restaurants offering northern Chinese food (wheat based), Xinjiang food (barbecue lamb), Sichuan based (spicy and hot pot based) and Cantonese food (rice and dim sum based). I had never tasted such a wide variety of Chinese regional food until I came to Shenzhen. For a person who is fond of trying various regional foods, then Shenzhen is the place to go. In fact, eating out in Shenzhen is now a favourite pastime for many people in Hong Kong who would take a day trip to Shenzhen to eat, before Covid-19 struck. In general, the cost of eating out is much cheaper in Shenzhen too. It does not mean Shenzhen offers no Western or Japanese style of cuisine, it is just not as common as in Hong Kong. Fast food such as McDonald's or Burger King is easily available in Shenzhen too. For me, having worked and lived in Shenzhen for the last nine years, I can hardly tell the difference when it comes to culinary expertise between Hong Kong and Shenzhen. Both have much to offer.

In summary, therefore, one would find it quite easy to conclude that there are more similarities than differences between the two cities. They are both very modern metropolises, and both are also looking to the future in working out the direction that they should take in the modern world.

The quality of life is therefore much the same and for me, Shenzhen may even have a slight edge. The main reason is that I work there. One always tends to favour the place of one's work, and I am no exception, plus the cost of living in Shenzhen on the whole is lower.

Both cities will play a pivotal part in the Greater Bay Area project in making the Pearl River Delta region a prosperous hub as a centre for most things, be it technology, services, commerce, or finance.

Therefore, I have always wondered, if I were asked again to give advice to the young in search of career prospects and business opportunities, whether I would try to broaden their path ahead for them by suggesting to them neither Hong Kong nor Shenzhen but the Greater Bay Area instead. It is important for the young to look wider and further in scope and vision. If one feels more comfortable in the world of Google, Amazon, Facebook, Netflix, YouTube and see them as a key component to enrich one's quality of life, then Hong Kong right now may be more preferable, at the price of a very high cost of living, driven up mainly by the often unaffordable property prices. On the other hand, if one is equally comfortable with Baidu, Alibaba, WeChat, Taoboa, Douyin (TikTok in China) and iQy (a popular streaming service in China, there are many other equally good streaming services too) as I am, then Shenzhen is equally good, if not better. One thing is sure though, that in the medium to long term (my estimate is five to ten years), the difference will be much less noticeable, and the Greater Bay Area by then would have passed the talking point stage and emerged as the clear winner, with the winning flag raised by the three brothers – Guangzhou, Shenzhen and Hong Kong!

A somewhat different line from a very famous film

Mum showed a box of chocolates to her son and said: 'Remember, son, life is like a box of chocolates, you never know what you are going to get!'

'But Mum,' replied the son, 'it is still a lovely chocolate, only with different fillings!'

www.ingramcontent.com/pod-product-compliance
Lightning Source LLC
Chambersburg PA
CBHW032116040426
42449CB00005B/163